Positive Behaviors *Start With* Positive Mindsets

Twenty-Eight Actions to
Motivate Students and Boost Achievement

TOM **HIERCK**   CHRIS **WEBER**

Copyright © 2025 by Solution Tree Press

Materials appearing here are copyrighted. With one exception, all rights are reserved. Readers may reproduce only those pages marked "Reproducible." Otherwise, no part of this book may be reproduced or transmitted in any form or by any means (electronic, photocopying, recording, or otherwise) without prior written permission of the publisher.

555 North Morton Street
Bloomington, IN 47404
800.733.6786 (toll free) / 812.336.7700
FAX: 812.336.7790

email: info@SolutionTree.com
SolutionTree.com

Visit **go.SolutionTree.com/behavior** to download the free reproducibles in this book.

Printed in the United States of America

Library of Congress Cataloging-in-Publication Data

Names: Weber, Chris (Chris A.) author. | Hierck, Tom, 1960- author.
Title: Positive behaviors start with positive mindsets : twenty-eight actions to motivate students and boost achievement / Chris Weber, Tom Hierck.
Other titles: 28 actions to motivate students and boost achievement
Description: Bloomington, IN : Solution Tree Press, [2024] | Includes bibliographical references and index.
Identifiers: LCCN 2024007528 (print) | LCCN 2024007529 (ebook) | ISBN 9781954631830 (paperback) | ISBN 9781954631847 (ebook)
Subjects: LCSH: Problem children--Education--United States. | Behavior disorders in children--United States. | Response to intervention (Learning disabled children)--United States. | Academic achievement--Psychological aspects. | Behavioral assessment of children. | Metacognition in children. | Behavior modification.
Classification: LCC LC4802 .W433 2024 (print) | LCC LC4802 (ebook) | DDC 371.930973--dc23/eng/20240515
LC record available at https://lccn.loc.gov/2024007528
LC ebook record available at https://lccn.loc.gov/2024007529

Solution Tree
Jeffrey C. Jones, CEO
Edmund M. Ackerman, President

Solution Tree Press
President and Publisher: Douglas M. Rife
Associate Publishers: Todd Brakke and Kendra Slayton
Editorial Director: Laurel Hecker
Art Director: Rian Anderson
Copy Chief: Jessi Finn
Proofreader: Elijah Oates
Text and Cover Designer: Laura Cox
Acquisitions Editors: Hilary Goff and Carol Collins
Content Development Specialist: Amy Rubenstein
Associate Editors: Sarah Ludwig and Elijah Oates
Editorial Assistant: Anne Marie Watkins

Acknowledgments

We would like to thank the incredible educators in Irvine Unified School District who embody the adult mindsets described in this book and who nurture the student mindsets that will lead to higher levels of behavioral and academic success in school, college, career, and life.

The examples provided in this book were created by the staff in Irvine Unified School District and are used with students every day to create supportive and engaging environments.

As authors, consultants, and educators, there is no better partner or publisher than Solution Tree. CEO Jeff Jones has been a mentor and friend for decades, and his leadership has truly helped transform education. Solution Tree Press president and publisher Douglas Rife is wise, kind, and so supportive of both Tom and Chris. Thanks to Tonya Cupp, again, for her outstanding editing; the extent to which this book is a polished product that provides optimal supports to educators is a credit to the incredible editing team at Solution Tree. Thank you so much to Shannon Ritz and Renee Marshall and their professional development and events teams for bringing our work and the work of other associates to districts, schools, and educators around the world.

We have been guided by the research around mindsets and noncognitive factors by Carol S. Dweck and Camille A. Farrington and their teams and are grateful for the practical contributions to our service to students that their work inspires. Lastly, we thank and miss Rick and Becky DuFour so much. Education is different and significantly better due to the incalculably positive impact of Professional Learning Communities at Work® on schools, educational leaders, and teacher teams.

Solution Tree Press would like to thank the following reviewers:

Kendra Bell
Educational Consultant
Peoria, Arizona

Doug Crowley
Assistant Principal
DeForest Area High School
DeForest, Wisconsin

Kristen Gibson
Instructional Specialist
Pasadena Independent
   School District
Pasadena, Texas

Ian Landy
District Principal of Technology
School District 47
Powell River,
   British Columbia, Canada

Kory Taylor
Reading Interventionist
Arkansas Virtual Academy
Little Rock, Arkansas

Visit **go.SolutionTree.com/behavior** to download the free reproducibles in this book.

Table of Contents

Reproducibles are in italics.

About the Authors vii

Introduction 1
    Parsing the Research 2
    Taking Action to Target Mindsets 3
    Navigating the Book 6

CHAPTER 1
"I Belong in This Academic Community" 9
    What Does "I Belong in This Academic Community" Mean? 10
    Why Focus on "I Belong in This Academic Community"? 10
    How Do We Nurture Students' Sense That "I Belong in This Academic Community"? . . 12
    Action Items 19
    Mindset Minilesson Design 20
    What I Want My Teacher to Know 21
    Interest and Connections Survey 22
    Classroom Environment Survey 23
    Student Input on Behaviors at Recess and Lunch 26
    Gratitude Journal Prompts 27
    Check-In/Check-Out Process 29
    "I Belong in This Academic Community" Action Plan 30

CHAPTER 2
"I Can Succeed at This" 33
  What Does "I Can Succeed at This" Mean? 34
  Why Focus on "I Can Succeed at This"? 38
  How Do We Nurture Students' Sense That "I Can Succeed at This"? 40
  Action Items 50
  Mindfulness Exercises 52
  "I Can Succeed at This" Action Plan 54

CHAPTER 3
"This Work Has Value for Me" 59
  What Does "This Work Has Value for Me" Mean? 59
  Why Focus on "This Work Has Value for Me"? 61
  How Do We Nurture Students' Sense That "This Work Has Value for Me"? ... 63
  Action Items 73
  "This Work Has Value for Me" Action Plan 75

CHAPTER 4
"My Ability and Competence Grow With My Effort" 79
  What Does "My Ability and Competence Grow With My Effort" Mean? 80
  Why Focus on "My Ability and Competence Grow With My Effort"? 83
  How Do We Nurture Students' Sense That "My Ability and Competence Grow With My Effort"? 84
  Action Items 89
  Growth Mindset Survey for Students 90
  Student Mindset Assessment for Teachers 91
  "My Ability and Competence Grow With My Effort" Action Plan 94

Epilogue 97

References and Resources 101

Index 113

About the Authors

Tom Hierck has been an educator since 1983 in a career that has spanned all grade levels and many roles in public education. His experiences as a teacher, an administrator, a district leader, a department of education project leader, and an executive director have provided a unique context for his education philosophy.

Tom is a compelling presenter, infusing his message of hope with strategies culled from the real world. He understands that educators face unprecedented challenges and knows which strategies will best serve learning communities. Tom has presented to schools and districts across North America with a message of celebration for educators seeking to make a difference in the lives of students. His dynamic presentations explore the importance of positive learning environments and the role of assessment to improve student learning. His belief that every student is a success story waiting to be told has led him to work with teachers and administrators to create positive school cultures and build effective relationships that facilitate learning for all students.

His most recent works include *Trauma-Sensitive Instruction: Creating a Safe and Predictable Classroom Environment* and *Trauma-Sensitive Leadership: Creating a Safe and Predictable School Environment* (both with John Eller) and *You're a Teacher Now! What's Next?* (with Alex Kajitani).

To learn more about Tom's work, visit his website at tomhierck.com or follow @thierck on X, formerly known as Twitter, or Tom Hierck on Facebook.

 **Chris Weber, EdD,** is an expert in behavior, mathematics, response to intervention (RTI), and multitiered system of supports (MTSS) who consults and presents internationally to audiences on important topics in education. As a teacher, principal, and curriculum director in California and Illinois, Chris worked with his colleagues to develop systems of supports that have led to high levels of learning at schools across the United States. In addition to writing and consulting, he continues to work as a principal in Irvine Unified School District in California, supporting some of the best and highest-performing schools in the country. Chris has been in service to community and country his entire life. A graduate of the U.S. Air Force Academy, he flew C-141s during his military career. He is also a former high school, middle school, and elementary school teacher and administrator. To learn more about Chris's work, visit Chris Weber Education (https://chriswebereducation.com) or follow @WeberEducation on X.

To book Tom Hierck or Chris Weber for professional development, contact pd@SolutionTree.com.

Introduction

Since the 2018 publication of Chris Weber's *Behavior: The Forgotten Curriculum*, we've seen that educators are increasingly committed to nurturing the critical behaviors that all students need to possess to be successful in school, college, career, and life. We've worked with schools across the United States, Canada, and Australia that have developed plans that systematically apply the principles of Professional Learning Communities (PLCs) at Work® and Response to Intervention (RTI) at Work™ to critical behavioral skills. These schools have consistently come to the same conclusion: positive behaviors begin with positive mindsets.

While educators have long acknowledged that promoting positive student behaviors is necessary so that we can get to the "real work" of academics, most now also embrace that behavioral skills are as important as, and perhaps even more important than, academic skills (Dweck, Walton, & Cohen, 2014). The postpandemic world has also seen an increase in educator concerns about student behaviors and an increased commitment to, and recognized need for, the teaching and learning of behaviors (Kuhfeld, Soland, Lewis, & Morton, 2022). These sets of desirable skills are sometimes known as *metacognitive skills*, *self-regulation*, or *executive functioning*. Regardless of the term used, these skills better predict success in school and beyond than test scores and intellectual ability, according to a wealth of research—including that of economists Lex Borghans, Bart H. H. Golsteyn, James J. Heckman, and John Eric Humphries (2016); researchers Angela L. Duckworth, Patrick D. Quinn, and Eli Tsukayama (2012); Duckworth and fellow psychologist Martin E. P. Seligman (2005); Heckman and fellow economist Tim Kautz (2012); psychologists Erik E. Noftle and Richard

W. Robins (2007); and researcher Arthur E. Poropat (2009). But crucial to this understanding of student success, according to Camille A. Farrington, senior research associate at the University of Chicago Consortium on School Research, and colleagues (2012) is that "the mechanisms through which teachers can lead students to exhibit greater perseverance and better academic behaviors in their classes are through attention to academic *mindsets* . . . rather than trying to change their innate tendency to persevere" (p. 7, emphasis added).

In the following pages of this introduction, we'll expand on these ideas, all the while conveying why a concerted effort to nurture specific mindsets among students is both essential and long overdue. Within this book, we'll describe the steps that educators in all schools can take to ensure that students possess the four positive mindsets that we'll explore here in depth, along with their associated behaviors: (1) "I belong in this academic community," (2) "I can succeed at this," (3) "This work has value for me," and (4) "My ability and competence grow with my effort" (Farrington et al., 2012, p. 9). Let's begin by taking a deeper dive into the compelling research on behaviors and mindsets before exploring how we can act on it. Then, we explain the book's structure and what you can expect from this resource.

Parsing the Research

This book rests on the comprehensive and definitive work in the field by Camille A. Farrington and colleagues (2012). Their research-based framework describes five interrelated categories of behavior—(1) mindsets, (2) social skills, (3) perseverance, (4) learning strategies, and (5) academic behaviors—which, in addition to mutually reinforcing one another and positively impacting academic achievement, are generally hierarchical.

1. **Mindsets:** Students feel a sense of belonging and belief. Students with positive mindsets will affirmatively respond to the following statements—the specific mindsets around which this book is based.

    - "I belong in this academic community." Students are connected to someone and something within school.
    - "I can succeed at this." Students believe they can achieve and have a positive sense of self-efficacy.
    - "This work has value for me." Students believe in the relevance of school, tasks, and experiences to their lives and futures.

- "My ability and competence grow with my effort." Students believe that they will make improvements with effort—that "smart" is something that you become, not something that you are.
2. **Social skills:** Students have respectful interactions with others and demonstrate respect for themselves; they cooperate and collaborate in appropriate ways and behave with empathy.
3. **Perseverance:** Students maintain effort and adapt to setbacks; they exercise self-discipline and self-control, delay gratification, and advocate for their needs.
4. **Learning strategies:** Students regulate, monitor, and reflect on their learning. They employ effective study and organizational skills, think metacognitively, and monitor their progress.
5. **Academic behaviors:** Students are physically, emotionally, and cognitively present and attentive while learning and within learning environments.

Certainly, while difficulties with displaying positive and productive academic behaviors will impact a student's mindsets, the flow of these behaviors occurs in a generally cause-and-effect way. A student with difficulties with noncognitive self-regulation is unlikely to possess positive mindsets. A student with compromised mindsets will be unlikely to display appropriate social skills. A student with inappropriate social skills will be unlikely to persevere. A student who does not persevere will be unlikely to practice productive learning strategies. And a student with unproductive learning strategies will be unlikely to display successful academic behaviors.

Mindsets, then, are the foundational sets of factors over which schools have significant influence, and mindsets are the factors or attributes that, when solidly and positively in place, will lead to student success with other behaviors, as well as with academics.

Taking Action to Target Mindsets

Defining behavioral skills in the context of Farrington and colleagues' (2012) framework is helpful because you can use their research and the five categories as an action plan. You can operationalize the research, putting these experts' best thinking into action and proactively supporting students as they develop skills when difficulties exist and when building a system of instruction and intervention. For example, say individual students are labeled as unmotivated—they don't seem to care about school, their grades, or their future. This is perhaps the most common concern that educators identify, particularly as students get older. A lack of motivation would appear as a deficit in the category of academic behaviors within the framework. The hierarchical nature of the framework reveals that there may also be predictable antecedents to poor academic behaviors or, more specifically, a lack of motivation.

Considering the framework from top to bottom, a student who is hungry, is tired, has difficulties modulating emotions, or has some combination of these needs may appear unmotivated and, more immediately, may not display positive, growth mindsets. A student without positive, growth mindsets may appear unmotivated and, more immediately, may not display positive social skills, which makes cooperating and collaborating with adults and students a challenge. A student lacking appropriate social skills may appear unmotivated and, more immediately, may not seem to persevere. A student who does not persevere may very well appear unmotivated and will be unlikely to employ productive learning strategies. Finally, a student who does not possess and use impactful learning strategies is unlikely to display appropriate academic behaviors and will appear to be, or may even be, unmotivated.

The point of these examples is to illustrate that there are reasons—explanations, causes, antecedents—to a student's difficulties with behavior. It all starts with mindsets. When as educators we consider behavioral skills within the context of Farrington and colleagues' (2012) framework, we can identify these reasons and do something about it. As John Seita (2014), associate professor of social work at Michigan State University, says, "Behavior is a form of communication providing clues about what is missing in a young person's life" (p. 30).

Student behavior is neither innate nor fixed. Educators can influence student behaviors—and we must. The research and studies cited throughout this book identify the skills students need to develop now; we know the behaviors that students must successfully display, and this book helps educators nurture them.

Educators know why schools need to focus on behaviors. Making time for the describing, modeling, teaching, practicing, and learning of behaviors is a challenge, but without reprioritizing those academic standards that are most critical for all students to learn, we cannot then carve out time and space for behavior teaching and learning and (specifically relevant to this book and foundational to all other behaviors) the nurturing of positive mindsets.

Mindsets are connected to, and foundational to, many of the other behavioral and social-emotional learning (SEL) initiatives with which your school district and school may be engaged.

- **Positive behavioral interventions and supports (PBIS):** The prosocial behaviors that PBIS promotes are consistent with the four mindsets. Schools that embrace the principles and practices of PBIS are committed to establishing and maintaining a positive school culture and productive student behaviors. Students' sense of belonging, sense of self-efficacy, belief in the relevance of school, and growth mindset are inextricably linked to schools' PBIS commitments. Your school's PBIS work (which includes mottoes such as "Respect, Responsibility, and Readiness" and "Be WISE," indicating a *w*inning attitude, *i*ntegrity, *s*hows of respect and responsibility, and *e*ncouraging others) is enriched when the four mindsets are explicitly woven into it.

- **SEL:** The Collaborative for Academic, Social, and Emotional Learning (CASEL, n.d.) identifies five competencies that are also consistent with and would be enriched by a commitment to nurturing student mindsets. These competencies—self-awareness, self-management, social awareness, relationship skills, and responsible decision making—developing depends on a student possessing a positive set of guiding mindsets.

- **Trauma-informed practices:** According to behavior analyst Jessica Minahan (2019), the core components of trauma-informed practices are as follows.
    - Expecting unexpected responses
    - Employing thoughtful interactions
    - Prioritizing relationship building
    - Promoting predictability and consistency
    - Teaching students how to avoid ruminating, or dwelling on the negative, by choosing a different task
    - Providing supportive feedback to reduce negative thinking
    - Creating places where struggling students feel competent (Brooks, 2003, as cited in Minahan, 2019)

> These actions are predicated on staff and students ensuring that students possess positive self-images and mindsets. Schools that commit to anticipating that they serve students who have or are experiencing traumas understand that belonging and self-efficacy are critical to healing and success.
>
> - **Social justice:** The first of the four domains of the social justice standards is *identity* (the other domains are diversity, justice, and action), and one's identity is significantly shaped by one's mindsets (Southern Poverty Law Center, 2018). A student's identities are multifaceted and central to how they behave and the extent to which they succeed and are fulfilled. Students have a stronger sense of belonging and see the relevance of school to a greater extent when their identities are represented and valued.

The behavioral skills that are critical to student success in school, college, career, and life are very likely connected to the work and initiatives with which your school is already engaged. In particular, it is critical to examine the extent to which mindsets are represented in your behavioral and SEL initiatives. Then, integrate the important work related to mindsets into daily practices. This book provides practical examples.

Navigating the Book

In our experience with schools, students struggle to grow behaviorally and in social-emotional domains during distance education; others echo this experience (Blad, 2022; Branje & Morris, 2021; Rodriguez-Monge, Isabela, & Chiappelli, 2023). While accessing academics in the absence of our brilliant teachers is not *better*, it's clear that it's possible to do. The same cannot be said for accessing and developing behavioral skills. Desired prosocial school behaviors are not cultivated in isolation or absent of interaction with others. Mindsets are foundational prerequisites to the development of behavioral skills.

K–12 educators who are committed to improving student engagement, motivation, behavior, and academic success can take action, introduce new ideas, and strengthen existing practices to ensure that all students possess positive mindsets. Each chapter of this book provides the information and recommendations that schools can use to achieve this goal for each of the four mindsets, which this book presents by chapter in sequence. We have experienced success introducing the mindsets to staff and students in the way described in the following paragraph, and the organization of the mindsets in this book reflects that decision.

Chapter 1, "'I Belong in This Academic Community,'" captures the mindset that ensures a student has a meaningful connection to the educational environment, a basic and fundamental sense of belonging. Chapter 2, "'I Can Succeed at This,'" covers the self-efficacy inherent in this critical student belief, the idea of hope and possibility. Chapter 3, "'This Work Has Value for Me,'" discusses the importance of imparting to students that what they're learning and experiencing in school will benefit them now and in the future. Chapter 4, "'My Ability and Competence Grow With My Effort,'" ends with a mindset essential to student success well beyond the classroom—one that realizes limitless personal growth and lifelong learning. Each chapter describes what it means to possess the mindset; shares research that validates why a focus on this mindset is essential; explains why a focus on the mindset belief is so critical to student success in school, college, career, and life; offers practical ways you can nurture the mindset, along with tips and resources for getting started and staying strong; and provides action items schools should consider as they initiate the work.

The conclusion offers practical examples for monitoring progress and celebrating success. Helping students develop positive mindsets *starts* with the adults on campus having positive mindsets themselves and committing to nurturing these mindsets in their students. This book is a resource to help educators make good on this commitment.

Learning Targets

By the end of this chapter, you'll be able to reflect positively on the following statements.

- I can identify and employ strategies and actions to ensure that adults intentionally connect with every student in my classroom and school.

- I can create environments and activities within which every student is connected to an adult, a peer, and a subject area or aspect of the school.

CHAPTER 1

"I Belong in This Academic Community"

How might you describe a "typical student" in a "typical classroom" in a "typical school"? You're right—it's a silly question. There is no such thing. Students come from various racial, ethnic, cultural, linguistic, and economic backgrounds. To model the mindset highlighted in this chapter, to create environments in which students feel cared for and connected, and to nurture in students a sense of belonging to their peers, the adults on campus, and the school itself, educators must keep in mind the incredible variety of students arriving at our schools and classrooms each day. While it would be impossible to be everything to every student, there is a need to enhance what it means for all students to feel like they belong. It's essential to acknowledge the lived experiences of students not only in the physical space of classrooms and schools but also in the instructional design and delivery of every educator. "I belong in this academic community" at a minimum implies that educators will create spaces and experiences in which all students recognize themselves and the myriad of possibilities that await them. This fundamental sense of belonging is truly the foundation of student success, as well as the precursor to acquiring the other mindsets of this book; without it, students may struggle with self-efficacy and motivation—something that even the most well-thought-out instructional strategies simply cannot contend with. So let's first take a closer look at what this mindset entails before exploring the research that supports our need to nurture it in students. Then, we look at concrete ways to help develop this mindset, as well as action items you can take individually and collectively in your school.

What Does "I Belong in This Academic Community" Mean?

According to researchers Ming Ming Chiu, Bonnie Wing-Yin Chow, Catherine McBride, and Stefan Thomas Mol (2016), a *sense of belonging* means that students are connected to something and someone at school and in the school community. That something may be an academic subject, a club, an activity, or a portion of the school day, and someone should include at least one adult and one peer. In capturing a sense of belonging, educators Kelly Allen, Margaret L. Kern, Dianne Vella-Brodrick, John Hattie, and Lea Waters (2018) convey that students should also feel as though they're accepted and liked by the rest of the group.

Learning in a school is a social endeavor during which students are learning with and from others. Schools are ultimately communities where educators strive to ensure students master content knowledge; when students feel connected to their peers and the adults at school, they are much more likely to feel like they belong in these academic communities and much more likely to possess the positive mindsets that lead to social and academic success (Farrington et al., 2012). Indeed, as developmental psychologist Andrew J. Fuligni (2019) notes, students should feel as though their identities—the identities to which they feel they belong—are valued, present, and represented within the school community. Students will feel as though they and the groups with which they identify are respected and that those groups matter. They'll see individuals from the groups and identities with which they identify represented in the school, the staff, and the subject areas they're learning; furthermore, as educational psychologist DeLeon L. Gray (2017) explains, they will see individuals from these groups and identities portrayed in a positive, successful light. When students believe that their environments are welcoming and affirming of who they are and those with whom they identify, and when they feel they are both welcomed and affirmed, they will feel a sense of belonging.

Why Focus on "I Belong in This Academic Community"?

According to Abraham Maslow (1943/2013), as well as educators Revathy Kumar, Akane Zusho, and Rhonda Bondie (2018), the extent to which students feel connected to their teachers, the content they're studying, their classmates, and the broader school community contributes to their behavioral, social-emotional, and academic success. Maslow's related work on hierarchical human needs and motivation is often represented as a pyramid, with physiological needs at the base. The following list reveals the order in which they must be satisfied—the first few are urgent.

1. Physiological needs
2. Safety
3. Belongingness and love
4. Self-esteem and achievement
5. Self-actualization

Schools have, since at least the 1990s and the founding of CASEL, more consistently worked to address physiological and physical safety issues in their learning environments (Jones & Doolittle, 2017). More frequently, however, the upper-level needs—achievement and self-actualization—continue to stand out as schools' primary and desired goals. How to get there often remains the challenge.

There is a critical gap in between that is often missed and yet is essential. As tempting as it is to jump straight to achievement and self-actualization, the representation by authors and educational consultants Floyd Cobb and John Krownapple (2019) shows the levels as a staircase. That staircase exemplifies how all the lower-level needs must be met before students can achieve higher-level goals. Expecting students to check their feelings at the door conflicts with their need to belong, in which case the goals of achievement and self-actualization may also elude their grasp.

The work of researcher Peter Bjorklund (2019) confirms that students who feel as though they belong, who feel as though they are accepted, and whose identities are both valued and represented, have higher senses of self-efficacy and higher levels of motivation. They are more confident in their identities and more willing to comply with established rules, norms, and expectations. They are more invested in learning and in school. They have more positive attitudes toward adults and students in the school. Researchers Kelly Ann O'Brien and Terry Vincent Bowles (2013) show that classroom contexts and educators can have a massive and positive impact on students' sense of belonging. Moreover, explain psychologists Gregory M. Walton and Shannon T. Brady (2017), staff-to-student and student-to-student relationships matter greatly in students' behavioral, social-emotional, and academic success. While both a strong sense of belonging and positive relationships improve outcomes for all students, they are particularly critical for our more vulnerable students (Bottiani, Bradshaw, & Mendelson, 2017; Gray, McElveen, Green, & Bryant, 2020).

Importantly, there are long-term benefits to positive teacher-student relationships and a strong sense of student belonging (Gopalan & Brady, 2020; Kim, 2021). This is particularly true for students from minority and historically marginalized groups (Murphy et al., 2020). We are committed not simply to telling students that they belong, but to showing them that they belong. The remainder of this chapter will provide practical ideas about how to do just that.

How Do We Nurture Students' Sense That "I Belong in This Academic Community"?

Nurturing students' sense of belonging will be positively impacted by the adults on campus taking steps to ensure that all students are more connected to someone and something at the school and that students "see themselves" in what they're learning and doing. Co-creating classroom norms (page 63) is one way to help increase belonging.

To this end, educators should attend to matters of social justice, the classroom environment, student-to-student relationships, teacher-to-student relationships, student participation in defining the expectations and operations of school and class, and student participation in clubs and activities. The sections that follow provide examples of how schools can further develop and nurture a sense of belonging in classrooms and other environments across campuses and describe why attending to each of these areas is important.

Strive for Social Justice

As discussed in the introduction, a student's identity is the first domain within the social justice standards and is central to a student's sense of belonging. The Southern Poverty Law Center (2018) created the social justice standards (twenty student attributes with the domains of identity, diversity, justice, and action) referred to in this book to promote tolerance and acceptance and ensure inclusivity for all students. That acceptance and inclusivity can lead to students feeling valued as individuals; when their identities are represented in classrooms and the school at large, they feel more connected to the school (Allen et al., 2018; Brady, Fryberg, & Shoda, 2018). The standards also encourage classrooms to have dialogue about who has power and who benefits from it, as well as what can change and how:

> However, classrooms can also shut down that conversation, whether it's in order to prepare for standardized tests, through a lack of discussion time, or because a teacher simply doesn't understand or value cultural competency. In order to foster classroom social justice, teachers must first build a safe, encouraging place where students can speak about their experiences and beliefs. (Blake, 2015)

In addition to allowing those conversations, ensure that student names are included in assignments and assessments. Ensure that students' cultures and varied lives are represented within resources and on the classroom walls. And while English may be the language of instruction in our classrooms, consider displaying ways of saying, "Good morning," "Hello," "Thank you," and other common phrases in languages represented in your school community. Equally important is to ensure that you correctly pronounce each student's name. Ask them to pronounce their names and record them, for yourself, phonetically. Ensure that students' identities (for example, race and ethnicity) and realities (for example, parents of the same gender or single parents) are represented within presentations and the instructional resources that are used within lessons.

Create a Greater Sense of Community and Comfort

Consider taking steps to create an even greater sense of community and comfort in the classroom. Soft starts and classroom meetings, two ideas that come from educator Harvey Daniels (2017), enhance the sense of community within a classroom and increase the sense of belonging students have to their teacher, their peers, and the class; these practices are validated by research on the importance of teacher-student relationships (Allen et al., 2018; Yu, Johnson, Deutsch, & Varga, 2018).

First, a few times a week, begin class with a soft start. When starting class with a soft start, students and the teacher engage in self-selected, nonacademic activities, perhaps reading, playing a game, completing a puzzle, pondering a quote you have written on the front board, or having a conversation, before academic work begins.

Second, engage in classroom meetings, in which students join the teacher seated on the carpet or standing in a circle around the perimeter of the room. In either case, there are several options: the day's agenda can be reviewed, individuals' social-emotional needs can be checked, the class can respond to a prompt (what is a trait about you that few may know and that you think is cool?), or expectations or a key behavioral or study skill can be reviewed and practiced. Meetings can occur regularly in an elementary classroom or during a middle or high school's homeroom class, or even periodically during a secondary classroom's language arts, mathematics, history, science, elective, or physical education class. In our experiences, dedicating time to this endeavor saves time later (given that behaviors, procedures, and expectations have been readdressed) and fosters more positive, productive learning environments.

Facilitate Positive Student-to-Student Relationships

Another way of increasing students' connectivity to each other and to the school is to initiate student mentors or buddy classrooms. Student mentors could involve assigning an upper-grade student to an individual or group of students from a lower grade (for example, a fifth-grade student to a kindergarten student, an eighth-grade student to a sixth-grade student, or a twelfth-grade student to a ninth-grade student). These mentors meet regularly with their assigned students to learn about one another and the school. Buddy classrooms may involve an entire fourth-grade class meeting with a first-grade class, or an eleventh-grade English class meeting with a ninth-grade English class (in the same period in the master schedule), to complete activities and reinforce the school's way of doing business.

One example from our work with elementary schools is fifth-grade students visiting their second-grade buddy classroom every month. Fifth graders are assigned a second grader with whom they meet for thirty minutes each visit, supporting the younger students as they revise and offer feedback about a writing assignment that the second graders have prepared in advance of the visit; of course, the fifth graders are also serving as models for appropriate social and academic behaviors. An example from secondary schools we've worked with includes eighth graders from a mathematics class visiting their sixth-grade buddies twice per trimester. The students work on a challenge assignment for a part of the period and answer questions about seventh and eighth grade during the other portion of the visit.

Both mentors and buddy classrooms connect students to students and strengthen the sense of belonging that students have to other students and to the broader school community (Graham, Wayne, Persutte-Manning, Pergantis, & Vaughan, 2022). They also provide insights to teachers who get to see their students operating in a different light in a mentoring role, providing teachers with the opportunity to model and observe skills and talents that may not have been visible in the classroom's daily routines.

Work on Positive Teacher-to-Student Relationships

Prioritize the building and nurturing of relationships between classroom teachers and their students within all classes and courses. Many students will not care to *know* an adult until they know that the adults *care*. This possibility of relating positively to others can be strengthened through the following actions, which signal to students that it's not just about academics—that the adult in the classroom also cares about each student as a person. In our professional experiences, intentionally nurturing stronger, more positive educator-student and student-student relationships is inextricably linked with students feeling a greater sense of belonging (California Safe and Supportive Schools & WestEd, 2020; Conner, Posner, & Nsowaa, 2022).

- **Classroom meetings:** As noted, meetings in elementary schools we have worked with occur three mornings a week in classrooms, with students sitting either on the carpet or at the perimeter of the room. In the secondary schools, these meetings occur once weekly. In both cases, teachers check in with students, students check in with one another, and everyone reinforces behaviors, procedures, and expectations. Through fostering a more positive and productive learning environment, students are more connected to their teacher and classmates. You can read more about them on page 13.

- **Mindset minilessons:** These minilessons are used as warm-ups several times a week, sometimes as part of the classroom meeting and sometimes as a lesson opener. The point is to explicitly teach about mindsets through examples of well-known public figures or through an age-appropriate review of the science. While this activity relates to some extent to all four of the mindsets described in this book, we find that students' sense of belonging is enhanced when they spend class time engaged in nonacademic tasks related to how their beliefs and attitudes impact their lives inside and outside of school. Figure 1.1 (page 16) offers an example minilesson, where students learn empathy. The reproducible "Mindset Minilesson Design" (page 20) is available, and you can visit **go.SolutionTree.com/behavior** to download a free version.

- **Student interest surveys:** At the beginning of the year and regularly throughout the year, ask students to complete a reproducible: "What I Want My Teacher to Know" (page 21) or "Interest and Connections

Learning target:
Students will demonstrate empathy when another student is having difficulty learning a new concept.
Success criteria:
The student in need will feel supported and hopeful. The supporting students will give time and attention to the student in need, using encouraging words and communicating about times when they have had difficulties learning new things.
Video or story to introduce the skill:
"Under the Surface" (Ayers, 2014)
Teacher modeling and explanation:
Teacher explains their own experiences in school—the difficulties and insecurities. Teacher describes how friends and adults helped.
Student practice in pairs or small groups:
Students take turns, in pairs, playing the student in need and supporting student in response to the following prompt: "A classmate is frustrated that they did not do well on a quiz even though they studied hard."
Check for understanding:
Each student writes one sentence in response to each of the following two questions: (1) How did it feel to be the student who didn't do well on the quiz? and (2) How did it feel to support a classmate?
Opportunities for application:
All teachers will embed opportunities for practicing empathy—through preteaching, reteaching, or connections to content—in each period throughout the week.

Source: © 2024 by Irvine Unified School District, Irvine, California. Used with permission.

Figure 1.1: Sample behavior minilesson.

Survey" (page 22). Teachers can use both resources with all students, although the first may be more appropriate for elementary students and the second more appropriate for secondary. These short surveys provide staff with information that will help ensure that students are connected to people and experiences at school and, when they may not be, will help staff connect students to staff and other students and will help them create opportunities to connect students to activities in which they have interests. We find students feel more connected to the adults at school and the school itself when the adults show a sincere interest in knowing more about them.

- **Environment surveys:** For a deep dive into a classroom's culture, use this type of survey to elicit feedback from students about what directly and indirectly influences student mindsets and many other attributes. We recommend using this survey approximately once a quarter. Teachers can individually examine the data to see if shifts are warranted in their classroom in response to student feedback to increase a sense of belonging. Collaborative teams can also share data and collaborate on ways to improve class culture. The following reproducibles align with this effort.

  - "Interest and Connections Survey" (page 22)—Teachers can also use this survey periodically throughout the year, perhaps in lieu of a classroom meeting, to learn more about their students and incorporate their interests into classroom meeting topics, assignments, and impromptu conversations.

  - "Classroom Environment Survey" (page 23)—Teachers can set aside time, perhaps in lieu of a classroom meeting, to have students complete the survey; they prepare them for it by reminding students to honestly share their opinions on the class and assuring them that they matter and that their input will make positive changes to the class. This survey is most appropriate for upper elementary and secondary students.

  - "Student Input on Behaviors at Recess and Lunch" (page 26)—Select and convene a group of students representing various student groups and levels of academic and social-behavioral success to gather feedback on what is going well, and not going as well, at the school.

- **Gratitude journals:** The reproducible "Gratitude Journal Prompts" (page 27) has ideas you can use in a lesson, typically at the beginning or end. Through practicing mindfulness, affirming a student's own value and worth, and expressing gratitude for their lives, we aim to guide students toward developing more positive mindsets—which research proves works (Brown & Wong, 2017; Del Castillo, 2022). These short activities help teach the power of mindsets and promoting positive mindsets early in a lesson.

- **Check-in/check-out:** Particularly for students about whom there are behavioral, academic, or social-emotional concerns, formalize check-in/check-out processes to connect with students with vulnerabilities and help them believe that they belong. This strategy involves setting goals with students, serving as a positive motivator for them, monitoring their improving behaviors, and providing strategies and tips for greater levels of behavioral and academic success. The reproducible "Check-In/Check-Out Process" (page 29) is available for use with this strategy.

Encourage Student Participation in Clubs and Activities

At all grade levels, find ways to provide opportunities for students to participate in activities that connect to their interests and passions. While this may look very different in kindergarten (where there may be choice time for students to explore their emerging age-appropriate interests), the upper-elementary grades, middle school, and high school (where teacher-led and student clubs can be organized into school schedules, during the day, or outside of school hours), participation in a club or activity that is a legitimate and honored part of the fabric of the school will increase a student's connection to school and therefore their sense of belonging. Research is clear: when students are involved in clubs, activities, and extracurricular activities, their success in school is enhanced (King, McQuarrie, & Brigham, 2021).

While this may challenge some students who have commitments outside of school, every effort should be made to ensure all students have an affiliation or connection to their school, and that this can occur within the hours of school time. One way to ensure that all students can take part is to ensure these activities occur within the school schedule. Building an exploration block into a school schedule is an example. A fixed period of time is part of the school schedule, and during that time, every adult in the building offers a topic of interest for which students can sign up. This also gives the adults an opportunity to share a personal interest or hobby with students.

We organize after-school arts; athletics; and science, technology, engineering, and mathematics (STEM) activities at our elementary schools so students can connect to school beyond the bell. In secondary schools, setting a goal and expectation that every student commits to an extracurricular activity is realistic and worthwhile. This expectation may challenge secondary schools in which some students do not currently have a match for their interests. The student interest surveys described earlier (page 15) can provide information that informs the offering of additional activities; the payoff will be worth it.

Action Items

When students feel truly connected to someone and something at school, they are much more likely to possess positive mindsets, much more likely to display appropriate behavioral skills, and much more likely to experience overall success in school. Taking active steps to promote a great sense of belonging is fundamental to promoting more positive mindsets.

At the conclusion of the chapter, we hope that you have been able to identify strategies and actions that ensure that adults on campus intentionally connect with every student in classrooms and across the school. We also hope that with this guidance you are able to develop strategies that help create environments and design tasks to connect every student to an adult, a peer, and a subject area or aspect of the school.

Having reflected on the importance of students being able to positively say, "I belong in this academic community," consider which of the following action items you can tackle individually or with your colleagues to nurture this mindset broadly.

- Review the suggestions within the chapter in comparison to what your school and district are already doing so that you can weave next steps into existing initiatives and commitments.

- Design or revise surveys or other information-gathering tools that allow students to report to whom and to what they are connected at school. Honor the information gathered in these surveys.

- Foster connections that students report to individuals and aspects of the school and provide opportunities for those connections to be strengthened.

- For students who are not yet connected to someone or something at the school, create systems that ensure they are connected to at least one adult, one peer, and one subject area or aspect of the school.

- Engage in professional learning—this book and its resource guides may help your efforts.

The reproducible "'I Belong in This Academic Community' Action Plan" (page 30) helps teams hold collaborative conversations, guided by this action plan, to reflect on where they are and identify next steps they can take.

Mindset Minilesson Design

Use or customize this basic outline when implementing a short lesson, warm-up, or classroom meeting. Choose a target that matches your school or classroom's mindset or behavioral area of focus or need. Then, complete the lesson using familiar elements of sound instructional design.

Learning target:

_____

_____

Success criteria:

_____

_____

Video or story to introduce the skill:

_____

_____

Teacher modeling and explanation:

_____

_____

Student practice in pairs or small groups:

_____

_____

Check for understanding:

_____

_____

Opportunities for application:

_____

_____

Source: © 2024 by Irvine Unified School District, Irvine, California. Used with permission.

What I Want My Teacher to Know

I wish you knew . . .

Finish this sentence with something you wish I knew about you. This could be something at home, a personal interest, a concern that you have about this school year, something you're excited for, the best way you learn, or anything else you feel safe sharing with me. (Only my eyes see this.)

Source: © 2024 by Irvine Unified School District, Irvine, California. Used with permission.

Interest and Connections Survey

Your answers will help us provide you opportunities that make school an even more fulfilling experience.

What staff person (teacher, vice principal, or librarian, for example) do you feel connected to and comfortable talking to?

_____
_____
_____
_____
_____

Please list students who you consider friends.

_____
_____
_____
_____
_____

What hobby, interest, or passion are you able to explore while at school?

_____
_____
_____
_____
_____

What hobby, interest, or passion do you *wish* you could explore while at school?

_____
_____
_____
_____
_____

Source: © 2024 by Irvine Unified School District, Irvine, California. Used with permission.

Classroom Environment Survey

This survey measures your classroom learning environment. It lets your teacher know what they can improve. Checkmark an answer for each statement, saying if each statement is:

- Totally untrue
- True just some of the time
- True most of the time
- Always true

	That is totally untrue.	That is true just some of the time.	That is true most of the time.	That is always true.
Student behavior in this class is under control.				
I hate the way that students behave in this class.				
Student behavior in this class makes the teacher angry.				
Student behavior in this class is a problem.				
My classmates behave the way my teacher wants them to.				
Students in this class treat the teacher with respect.				
Our class stays busy and doesn't waste time.				
If we don't understand something, my teacher explains it a different way.				
My teacher knows when the class understands and when we do not.				

	That is totally untrue.	That is true just some of the time.	That is true most of the time.	That is always true.
My teacher has several good ways to explain each topic that we cover in this class.				
My teacher explains difficult things clearly.				
My teacher asks questions to be sure we are following along when they are teaching.				
My teacher asks students to explain more about the answers they give.				
In this class, my teacher accepts nothing less than our full effort.				
My teacher doesn't let people give up when work gets hard.				
My teacher wants us to use our thinking skills, not just memorize things.				
In this class, we learn every day.				
My teacher asks students to explain more about the answers they give.				
In this class, we learn to correct our mistakes.				
This class does not keep my attention, and I get bored.				

	That is totally untrue.	That is true just some of the time.	That is true most of the time.	That is always true.
My teacher makes learning enjoyable.				
I like the ways we learn in class.				
My teacher takes time to summarize what we learn each day.				
My teacher checks to make sure we understand what they are teaching us.				
We get helpful comments to let us know what we did wrong on assignments.				
The comments that I get on my work in this class help me understand how to improve.				

What else would you like your teacher to know about your experience in this class?

You may share your name if you would like your teacher to know who you are or if your final comments need your teacher to know who you are to better understand or address concerns or enjoyments in this class.

Source: © 2024 by Irvine Unified School District, Irvine, California. Used with permission.

Student Input on Behaviors at Recess and Lunch

What is something that is going *well* out at recess and lunch?
Why do you think it's going well?
What is something we need to work on outside at recess and lunch?
Why is this something that we need to work on?
What do you think would help?
What can we do to help out at recess and lunch?
What can your teachers do to help out at recess and lunch?
Do you think students know how to tell an adult if there's a problem? Do you think students do this?
What's a topic (for example, bad language or disrespect) that you think we should focus on?

Source: © 2024 by Irvine Unified School District, Irvine, California. Used with permission.

Gratitude Journal Prompts

Journaling about gratitude helps students work toward the "I belong in this academic community" and "I can succeed at this" mindsets (Farrington et al., 2012, p. 9).

Think-Draw-Write

Answer the following questions. Illustrate or write your answers.

- Think of a time you learned something new outside of school. What steps did you take to learn it?
- Think of a time you failed at something. What happened after you failed?

The Two Brains

With words and images, create a fixed mindset brain and a growth mindset brain. Ask students to explain their creations in pairs. Select a random student pair to share the key attributes of a fixed and growth mindset.

How Learning Target Trackers Help Us

Think about your learning target tracker and then answer the following questions.

- Why do we use learning target trackers?
- How can a learning target tracker help you in class?
- How does a learning target tracker support a growth mindset?

Myths and Truths About Learning

Answer the following questions.

- Do you believe that successful students ever ask questions?
- What resources could you use in addition to listening in class and asking the teacher for clarification?
- Do you feel confident about how you study for tests? Are you getting the results that you want?
- If not, how could you get better at studying?
- Would getting better at studying help you achieve the results you want?
- If not, why not?

Reference

Farrington, C. A., Roderick, M., Allensworth, E., Nagaoka, J., Keyes, T. S., Johnson, D. W., et al. (2012). *Teaching adolescents to become learners. The role of noncognitive factors in shaping school performance: A critical literature review.* Accessed at https://consortium.uchicago.edu/sites/default/files/2018-10/Noncognitive%20Report_0.pdf on November 13, 2023.

Thanks, Friend

Write a letter to a friend or teacher and say why you appreciate them.

Smashing Stereotypes

Write a paragraph or draw a picture that shows how an assignment, your classroom environment, an assessment, or the school campus allows you to see yourself and your culture represented.

Source: © 2024 by Irvine Unified School District, Irvine, California. Used with permission.

Check-In/Check-Out Process

Check-in/check-out for (student) _____

Check-in/check-out with (staff) _____

Date: _____

Today, I am working on: _____
(Target behavior with specific description if necessary)

Focus strategy: _____
(Strategy that matches target behavior)

This is how I did today:

- 3—Great (I was reminded to be on task one time.)
- 2—Pretty well (I was reminded to be on task two or three times.)
- 1—So-so (I was reminded to be on task more than three times.)

Times of the Day	Target Behavior	
	Student	Staff

Today, I earned _____ points.

_____ points or more = _____

Parent signature: _____

Source: Weber, C. (2018). Behavior: The forgotten curriculum. An RTI approach for nurturing essential life skills. Bloomington, IN: Solution Tree Press.

"I Belong in This Academic Community" Action Plan

Among your collaborative teams, discuss these issues and create plans to address the ideas and suggestions recommended in this chapter.

Possible Action Area	Progress-Monitoring Suggestion	Next Steps
Social Justice In what ways can curriculum, instruction, and assessment be customized to reflect the ways in which students see themselves?	Examine assignments, resources, and assessments quarterly to determine whether these items increasingly represent students' cultures, languages, and lives.	
Classroom Environment In what ways can the plans for how time and space are used within the classroom (or school) be altered to help students feel a greater sense of belonging?	Analyze the results of the student surveys in this book to determine if students feel a sense of connectedness and belonging.	

page 1 of 2

REPRODUCIBLE

Possible Action Area	Progress-Monitoring Suggestion	Next Steps
Student-to-Student Relationships — What steps can be taken to more positively connect students within the classroom, within the grade level, and across the school to one another?	Analyze the results of the surveys in this book to determine whether students' relationships with classmates and other peers are healthy or improving.	
Teacher-to-Student Relationships — What steps can be taken to get to know students even more and let students get to know their teachers?	Analyze the results of the surveys in this book to determine if students' feelings toward the adults on campus are healthy or improving.	
Student Participation in Clubs and Activities — How can the school ensure that all students are connected to at least one aspect of the school environment (a content area, a club, an extracurricular)?	Collect and analyze data on the percentage of students involved in extracurricular activities.	

page 2 of 2

Positive Behaviors Start With Positive Mindsets © 2024 Solution Tree Press • SolutionTree.com
Visit **go.SolutionTree.com/behavior** to download this free reproducible.

Learning Targets

By the end of this chapter, you'll be able to reflect positively on the following statements.

- I can foster higher levels of self-efficacy.
- I can develop academic perseverance in my students.
- I can define success and contextualize it in various academic and social situations for my students.

CHAPTER 2

"I Can Succeed at This"

When students and staff believe they can do something, they are much more likely to be successful at doing that thing. Research bears this out, for psychologist Albert Bandura (1977), who established the concept of self-efficacy, is attributed with saying, "People's beliefs about their abilities have a profound effect on those abilities." This assertion has been validated in a number of subsequent research studies looking at the impact of educators believing in themselves and their students having a positive impact on outcomes (Cohen & Garcia, 2014; Dweck, 2013; Geers, Weiland, Kosbab, Landry, & Helfer, 2005; Goddard, Hoy, & Hoy, 2004).

Maslow's hierarchy of needs takes this a step further. The essence of "I can succeed at this" derives from what Maslow (1943/2013) described as our basic "need or desire for a stable, firmly based, (usually) high evaluation of [our]selves, for self-respect, or self-esteem, and for the esteem of others" (p. 7). A translated quote by Virgil (70–19 BC, line 231)—"They can, because they think they can"—seems simple but is layered in complexity and at the core of the work we do as educators. It's also a significant reminder to ourselves that we have the capacity to do great things, and that often begins with a belief that we are able.

Every educator has probably known students with lower confidence levels and observed that their levels of engagement in tasks related to a given topic, their willingness to stretch and take risks, and their ultimate success are compromised when they do not believe they can succeed. Psychologists often call this *self-efficacy* while many of our educator colleagues will simplify it to "believing in yourself." Either way, it's a necessary and practical frame of mind that empowers all learners to make positive progress. When students believe in their ability to succeed in tasks, even when the tasks are challenging, this belief and mindset impacts their ability to persist and accomplish those challenging tasks.

As educators work to create learning opportunities for students, it should be with an eye toward helping them to set goals, receive feedback, and reflect on their progress. This can positively impact their beliefs about their abilities and their expectations of success.

As you read through this chapter, reflect on what you and your team can do to foster this mindset. When students believe they are "good" or can be "good" at a particular kind of task or learning target, there is a strong association with positive mindsets, academic perseverance, and, ultimately, better academic performance. Let's take a look at what "I can succeed at this" entails, explore the why behind nurturing this mindset among students, consider practical ways to help solidify this mindset among students, and review related action items you can take individually and collectively in your school.

What Does "I Can Succeed at This" Mean?

This mindset is built on two foundational aspects: (1) teachers' mindsets about success and (2) the students' beliefs in themselves. Teachers' mindsets have a major impact. Research shows that sharing the simple sentence, "I am giving you this feedback because I believe in you," corresponds with students who scored academically higher the following year (Cohen & Garcia, 2014). Teachers' words and the beliefs they hold about students help to develop these positive, and ongoing, outcomes.

Now, imagine these two student progress scenarios: Student A consistently achieves the highest grade on any assignment or assessment. This student arrived to their current grade reading above level and continues to score above grade level. Student B has had varying degrees of success on assignments and assessments. This student arrived to their current grade at least two levels behind in reading and has shown significant growth, gaining eighteen months in their reading level, but is still not yet where they need to be. Which of these students would fit your definition, as an educator, of success? How would you justify your answer?

Both students (and most students in schools) are models of success. However, if we limit our definition of success to a score or a comparison to other students in the same class, we may miss out on the multitude of demonstrations of success evident in schools today. The COVID-19 pandemic highlighted some of the challenges schools face that were not as evident prior to the pandemic. We have heard from colleagues about students who demonstrated talents and abilities that were not noticed in a typical structured classroom but became evident during remote learning or when students could show their learning in other ways. Each student is unique. The homogeneity that is sometimes assumed based on the "traditional" students of the past, all generally receiving the same form of instructional design and delivery, may well not be seen again.

As mentioned, educators have typically measured student success by grades on a report card or year-end transcript. The current realities in schools undermine this "typical year" or "typical student" approach, and success for many students will continue to look very different. Some of them will further refine their technology skills, producing success measured in metrics associated with positive acknowledgements of the information they shared. Neither of this book's authors grew up in a time where internet personality was a career option, for example, but that is now a viable option for students. Typical is gone.

This is not a negative development, and may even be cause for celebration, as educators continue to embrace the variety of learning styles and learners before them each day. By the way, these were not new skills developed in response to the pandemic but more likely overlooked skills that became necessary during the pandemic. For example, for some of our students, their families, and even our colleagues, surviving school during the pandemic further developed the skills of resiliency and added additional coping strategies. Those skills may have been dormant in previous school models, and their emerged relevancy will serve our students well in whatever they attempt next. As we talk about in chapter 4 (page 79), the sum total of the thirteen-year experience we call school is ideally designed to open doors. Instead of funneling to one option (often college entrance), it instead should open to a variety of options all deemed worthwhile and considered success.

Success, then, needs to have a broader definition that incorporates both the short-term (immediate) goals of students and the long-term (future) aspirations of students and the school systems that support them. Society may view high school graduation as a worthy indicator of success while also recognizing that there are different pathways and time periods that each student will take to achieve that end goal. As you ponder this notion, think about your own success. Did you get better at any skill or learning target as an adult than you demonstrated as a student? If we hold to the premise that school is a thirteen-year experience, and not thirteen ten-month experiences, would our definition of success be broadened?

When asked what attributes educators would like every student to have at the end of their thirteen years of school, the list is likely to consistently include confidence, perseverance, kindness, empathy, and self-awareness, as well as being a self-starter, communicator, and hard worker. When the same question is posed to a grade-level audience, educators may tend to default to specific learning targets of the course at that grade level. Can you see how looking at an entire experience over a decade of schooling versus a particular ten-month segment would shift the views of success? The latter often results in a view of success based on performance levels, while the former speaks to measures of success achievable by all students in the grade level, with the academic content being the vehicle with which those attributes can be achieved. Educators must always account for the former when considering student success. Taking to heart this nuanced understanding of success then becomes the means by which we can immediately empower students. We can do this by emphasizing growth versus achievement and the importance of *yet*.

Growth Versus Achievement

As educators wrestle with views of success as outlined previously, it's equally important to discuss what we're measuring. Is it achievement (how students perform at one point in time) or growth (the amount of academic progress students make between two points in time)? Are we concerned about status or progress? Tom Hierck and Angela Freese (2018) define *status* (achievement) as the "moment of proficiency, a student's progress relative to the threshold (the bar or better) or expectation that has been defined" (p. 108). They define *progress* (growth) as the "moments before proficiency and beyond proficiency, for those students not there yet and for those students beyond" (Hierck & Freese, 2018, p. 108).

To build the mindset of "I can succeed at this," our students need to know that success is possible even if it is not evident in the moment. There are some limitations to simply aiming for achievement (status), including that these data may give an inaccurate picture of what students can do, particularly for those students who might have accelerated beyond the goal. Secondarily, if a status goal is linked to an assessment that students take only once, does this mean that educators offer only one opportunity for students to demonstrate proficiency? This would undermine the notion of learning from failure and would definitely inhibit the development of the mindset focused on in this chapter, as success would be reduced to an all-or-nothing proposition based on the outcome of a single measure. If educators shift to growth (progress) goals, then the focus becomes improving students' learning and achievement and building their capacity to learn. This shift is really, in many ways, personal to the student and based on their current standing academically and behaviorally. When educators focus on individual growth rather than an expectation driven by age and grade, they can differentiate to meet the needs of their students. The authors look at rigor as being that place just beyond where a student currently resides, as in psychologist Lev Vygotsky's (1978) zone of proximal development (ZPD)—an area that exists between what a learner can do without assistance and what a learner can do with adult guidance or in collaboration with more capable peers. In other words, rigor is available to all students from kindergarten to grade 12, from our most accelerated learners to our learners who are not anywhere near proficient. This implies that teachers will work with students from where they are and takes them to that tangible growth. This should involve plans to differentiate instruction to ensure the needs of the diverse learners who populate our classrooms today are met. We can control this; as Hierck and Freese (2018) suggest, educators should "plan for *all* students to at least attain proficiency and for some to move beyond proficiency in a meaningful, challenging way" (p. 108). If we want all students to be engaged and motivated and to give their best—whether they are not yet at proficiency, at proficiency, or above proficiency—then committing to promoting more positive mindsets is key.

The Importance of Yet

Arguably, one of the simplest ways educators can promote the mindset of "I can succeed at this" is through the use of this simple three-letter word—*yet*. For students who are struggling to achieve the desired learning outcomes (the "need to know" as defined by the grade level or content team), we need to make it clear that there is still the possibility for them to achieve those goals, and that we are committed to helping those students achieve them. Every time students voice a common refrain—"I can't do this"—complete the sentence for them with this powerful three-letter word. This must be held firm, particularly if educators have described a learning target as essential. As Hierck (2017) points out, "There are no other options available, and holding students and teachers accountable for achieving the desired outcomes has to be part of every classroom" (p. 61). As we build this mindset, it's also important to remember that the achievement does not have to happen all at once, but it must eventually happen on those learning targets deemed to be priorities. This aligns well with the ZPD, which speaks to growth over time (Vygotsky, 1978).

Why Focus on "I Can Succeed at This"?

For us as two educators with a combined experience of more than sixty years, this scenario plays out time and again: if students believe they can complete a particular task or succeed in a course of study, there is a strong connection to their staying committed to the task—to their academic perseverance. The mindset of "I can succeed at this" is a powerful attribute for all students to develop and for all educators to cultivate. For students to expend the sustained effort necessary for learning, they must believe their efforts will be successful. Research shows that self-efficacy and the belief in one's likelihood of success are generally more predictive of academic performance than one's actual measured ability.

The work of psychologists Albert Bandura (1986) and Daphna Oyserman and Leah James (2009) confirms that individuals more willingly engage in tasks of any kind when they anticipate success. Farrington and colleagues (2012) suggest:

> When students believe they are likely to succeed in meeting academic demands in a classroom, they are much more likely to try hard and to persevere in completing academic tasks, even if they find the work challenging or do not experience immediate success. (p. 29)

Research on effect size shows that student self-efficacy is a very effective strategy that educators can employ to significantly, and positively, impact student outcomes. Remember, a typical year of instruction has an effect size of 0.40, which is connected to a year's growth. A 0.71 indicates that the expected growth for students could be almost *two times higher* as a result. In other words, believing one can be successful is a prerequisite to putting forth the required effort and sustaining that effort. Couple this with students valuing the work (as discussed in chapter 3, page 59), and educators can better influence the persistence and performance of their students.

The negative impact when there is an absence of this mindset is significant. Students' academic experiences shape their academic beliefs and behaviors. This gets further compounded by factors such as grade level, prior academic achievement, English learner status, and race or ethnicity. In a report for the Institute of Education Sciences, Jason Snipes and Loan Tran (2017) offer this insight:

> Growth mindset scores were 0.2–0.8 standard deviation lower for students with lower prior academic achievement, English learner students, and Black students than for their higher achieving, non–English learner, and White counterparts. Performance avoidance scores were higher for students with lower prior academic achievement, English learner students, and Black students. (p. i)

Research also suggests that challenges exist with students from lower-income families in developing this (or any other) positive mindset. Susana Claro, David Paunesku, and Carol S. Dweck (2016) explain that "economic disadvantage may lead to poorer academic outcomes, in part by leading low-income students to believe that they cannot grow their intellectual abilities" (p. 8667). But the good news these researchers uncovered should encourage all educators in the relentless pursuit of developing this mindset: "At every socioeconomic level, those who hold more of a growth mindset consistently outperform those who do not—even after holding constant a panoply of socioeconomic and attitudinal factors" (Claro et al., 2016, p. 8667). If we are aware that students have barriers to success that exist outside of school—and the evidence of this reality exists for virtually every student—we must commit to cultivating the mindset "I can succeed at this." Ultimately, educators must determine if they are gathering formal and informal evidence—assessment data, surveys, observations, and more—to make plans (build the mindset) or to make excuses (and reinforce the misguided notion that growth is not possible).

One final piece of research is linked to the idea that students who believe they have the competence to succeed show greater motivation, greater perseverance, and more effective study strategies. This notion of self-efficacy—a mindset of "I can succeed at this"—is described by Ellen L. Usher and Frank Pajares (as cited by Chew, 2022) as having three sources, which they identify as:

> mastery experiences, vicarious experiences, and verbal and social persuasion. In mastery experiences, students succeed at a course-related task. Vicarious experiences occur when students observe or learn about other students who have succeeded. Verbal and social persuasion occurs when the instructor or peers give encouragement or help.

As you think about these three definitions, consider the following questions.

- What can you plan for in your instructional design and delivery?
- How might you build success opportunities for all students, from your most able and successful learners to your most "not yet" students?
- What authentic encouragement can you provide to students at varying points on the learning continuum?

From their first interactions with students, teachers can be encouraging as they discuss what students in previous classes experienced and what they did to succeed. They can also promote those behavioral norms that will help students be successful and model those norms so students see what success looks like.

When improvement happens gradually over time, as it most often does, it may be hard for students (and their teachers) to see the growth. If educators are intentional about reflecting on growth and sharing both strengths and stretches (lessons to be learned), they can help students build confidence and ownership.

How Do We Nurture Students' Sense That "I Can Succeed at This"?

Teachers have a strong influence over all the academic mindsets via their instructional design and delivery and by creating environments that shape students' motivation, engagement, and persistence (Allensworth et al., 2018). As discussed in chapter 1 (page 9), it is critical that educators create a sense of belonging and ensure classrooms are places of emotional safety. This section examines other ways that educators can nurture the mindset of "I can succeed at this" while also ensuring students continue to progress forward in achieving all their behavioral and academic outcomes. Two ways that educators can incorporate this mindset are (1) setting high expectations and (2) framing mistakes as an important part of learning. Let's examine each of these separately.

Hold High Expectations

Teachers can help students develop the mindset of "I can succeed at this" by nurturing a positive developmental relationship in which they both support and challenge students (California Safe and Supportive Schools & WestEd, 2020; Cohen & Steele, 2002; Farrington et al., 2012). A central way to do this is by setting high expectations. Educators often share the notion that all students can learn. While there is no doubt about the sincerity or the intent with which this message is delivered, there can be unintentional misalignment between this statement and the practices observed in classrooms. Do the policies, procedures, and practices of the classroom (and, by extension, the school at large) match this desired outcome? Visit https://tinyurl.com/2kwee2nh to access the High Expectations Self-Assessment Checklist from the Education Hub. Staff can use this self-assessment to learn how they can enhance the extent to which all students believe that the adults on campus have high expectations for their success, identify practices they already have established (and that they should continue), and determine possible next steps.

As we ponder what it means to behave in a way that validates the belief that all students can learn, professor John Hattie (2012) in *Visible Learning for Teachers: Maximizing Impact on Learning* suggests that it is obvious when educators are inspired by the belief when he states:

> There are certainly many things that inspired teachers do *not* do; they do *not* use grading as punishment; they do *not* conflate behavioural and academic performance; they do *not* elevate quiet compliance over academic work; they do *not* excessively use worksheets; they do *not* have low expectations and keep defending low-quality learning as "doing your best"; they do *not* evaluate their impact by compliance, covering the curriculum, or conceiving explanations as to why they have little or no impact on their students; and they do *not* prefer perfection in homework over risk-taking that involves mistakes. (p. 32)

Similarly, teachers who have *low expectations* of their students display certain behaviors that clearly undermine the belief that all students can learn. Educators identify the following list of attributes that are evident in teachers with low expectations for their students (Rubie-Davies, Peterson, Sibley, & Rosenthal, 2015). Avoid these behaviors.

- Using ability grouping for activities
- Rarely providing students with choice
- Asking more closed- rather than open-ended questions
- Praising or criticizing students based on accuracy
- Asking other students for the correct answer when a student answers incorrectly, rather than trying responses that might draw out the student's thinking
- Managing behavior reactively

How can we shift this focus and become more aligned between our beliefs and our behaviors? We should create experiences that allow and require students to work to mastery. We should create opportunities for students to see other students' progress and succeed and highlight it and leverage the power of peer modeling. We ought to provide meaningful feedback signaling that we care and believe all students are progressing. Letting them know (and believing it yourself); allowing voice and choice; giving specific feedback; adopting a growth mindset; and making expectations clear, realistic, and reasonable are other strategies for teachers to consider.

Let Them Know (and Believe It Yourself)

Let students know that you believe in them and their capacity to learn. Remember that most important three-letter word—*yet*—when students doubt their ability. Be honest with them about the challenges before them. Engage your students through nonverbal signals such as smiling and nodding to give encouragement. Also, speak positively about your students to other staff, including the ones whom you know struggle. Find some asset that a student possesses rather than agreeing with the negative portrayal that might be the common, accepted view of the student.

Allow Voice and Choice

When students are given a chance to voice their opinions and learning in a validating atmosphere, they learn better and achieve higher results (Conner et al., 2022). When students have a say and have options in their school lives, they are more likely to see that school is relevant because it is not something that is done to them—it's something to which they contribute.

Some ideas for increasing student voice and choice are listed here (and are meant not to be exhaustive, but to offer some avenues to explore).

- **Policy and practice:** One of the authors (Tom) worked in a district leadership role where students from all schools were invited to help shape the district and community policy. For example, one of the sessions focused on graffiti around town. Schools sent a variety of students (and not always their highest achieving), and the student voice significantly helped determine future actions.

- **Classroom expectations:** Teachers can cocreate with students the expectations for the year and how everyone will operate as the year unfolds. Giving voice to what needs to happen for the class to function effectively invites great dialogue. It also helps ensure that students know what is expected of them, which results in "students who are: on-task at higher rates, have more prosocial behaviors with peers, and overall are more academically successful" (Croce & Salter, 2022, p. 1).

- **Literature:** An easy way to engage student choice is by offering them just that when it comes to the books they read for school assignments. Perhaps it is time to move beyond works written by 16th century white males to those novels that might have greater appeal to students today and might resonate deeper in their lives. This is not to suggest all of the literary classics be abandoned in one quick decision, but it is to exercise options to engage students in a necessary lifelong skill—reading!

- **Physical education:** Physical education is always a challenge for students who view themselves as nonathletic or who are going through times in their lives when they are body aware. Others may not like the notion of changing into appropriate gym wear. One school addressed these concerns by having the school schedule structured to have physical education at the same time for three classes of students and then have the three teachers offer a different option for the activities of the class. Students chose what activity they would prefer to participate in for that unit. This significantly and positively impacted the challenges seen previously.

Give Specific Feedback

Individualized feedback (not simply *Good job!*) has one of the highest effect sizes on student achievement, allowing students to use the feedback to improve; the key components of feedback follow (Hattie, 2023).

- Timely
- Specific
- Personalized rather than generalized

Specific feedback drives improvement for all students (Hattie & Gan, 2011).

Larry Ainsworth and Donald Viegut (2006) suggest the following ideas for what to do with assessments.

- **Diagnose student learning difficulties:** High-quality, team-developed formative and summative assessments will give great insights into student successes and yet-to-be mastered learning targets.
- **Set individual teacher goals for student improvement:** Being a member of a collaborative team implies that educators have a common purpose (all students learning at high levels, for example) and will adopt an unrelenting focus on that purpose. Being vulnerable with colleagues means an expectation that all educators will accept responsibility for the results and work to improve them.
- **Set team goals for student improvement:** Adopting the view that all students will be proficient should be the goal for all teacher teams.

As the next bullet explains, this is based on conversations about what worked and how educators can move forward.

- **Identify and share effective instructional strategies:** When teacher teams gather to look at the results of their common assessments and align those results with their individual instructional design and delivery, the conversation can focus on what worked for which students and what happens next in terms of intervention to close gaps.
- **Plan differentiated instruction:** Once the conversations have occurred, teachers can determine the next steps for differentiation, including which teacher will be responsible for this and when it will occur for the student (during class or in a separate period).

Adopt a Growth Mindset

This involves focusing on the value of the process and focused efforts that contribute to achieving proficiency, rather than the outcome. With a growth mindset, educators have high expectations for the effort that goes into study and learning, whereas a fixed mindset focuses on getting good grades—the outcome. Cultivate a growth mindset in your students by emphasizing the importance of hard work—as the key to learning more, as the path to achieving good grades, and as something of value in and of itself. There is more on this in chapter 4 (page 79).

Make Expectations Clear, Realistic, and Reasonable

Many students become overwhelmed by pressure because they don't know exactly what is expected of them. Setting clear, achievable expectations for your students and making sure they know exactly what expectations are, and how you expect all students to achieve them, is not giving them the answers—it's sharing the process to get to the desired outcomes. Again, the focus is on the process, rather than the outcome. Provide clear examples of high-quality work and express confidence that students can perform to that standard (Osher & Kendziora, 2010). It may mean explicitly asking language arts students, "Cite three pieces of evidence from the text to defend your position," or it may be as subtle as suggesting that the current text and the previous text might involve more than one potential defense of their view. Think, for example, of a narrative written from an opposite viewpoint than what you might traditionally have been exposed to (the Three Little Pigs story written from the viewpoint of the Big Bad Wolf). In mathematics this might mean showing all the steps in solving a problem, or it may mean asking students to identify an alternate way to get the result other than the method demonstrated by the teacher.

Educators often lament, "But my students need to have rigor in their learning!" Here's a definition of *rigor* that allows for that concern to be addressed while also embracing the mindset we are focused on—rigor is that place just beyond where the student currently resides. In this definition, rigor is available at every grade level, to your highest-achieving student and to your most "not yet" student. All students grow from their current place to the next place in their learning continuum. This also aligns with the oft-desired goal of lifelong learning.

As mentioned, The Education Hub has created a High Expectations Self-Assessment Checklist (http://tinyurl.com/2kwee2nh) that describes teacher actions aligned with creating this environment. It is based on the work of professor Christine M. Rubie-Davies and colleagues (2015) and includes some of the strategies identified previously, including feedback, goal setting, and formative assessment. While the intent is for students to use this tool to self-assess, educators may also want to work with a colleague and collaboratively support each other while setting some growth goals for themselves.

Frame Mistakes and Struggle as Normal and Productive

Students are expected to be competent enough to independently fulfill all their class- or content-identified outcomes, both academically and behaviorally. If educators help too much, they may send the message that the expectations are low and that students can't rise to the levels set by their teacher. Failure is part of the process, but educators often grade with a single-chance mindset. If we want students to learn that failure is a part of growth, to be motivated by their mistakes, to discover where they went wrong, and to strive to fix errors, they must see the adults model that. Failure is discussed as part of the mindset in chapter 4, "My Ability and Competence Grow With My Effort."

Allow for productive struggle and provide guidance and support for students when they engage with challenging material without jumping in with the answers. We, the authors, have worked with many teachers who employed the Three Before Me strategy rather than always responding each time a student raises their hand. This strategy is based on the notion that a student will try three other sources of possible solution gathering—peers, books in the room, information on the board or classroom walls, for example—before getting assistance from the teacher. If a teacher responds every time a student raises their hand, students will become accustomed to the quick, easy solution, which undermines the capacity to internalize this mindset (and learn self-reliance). While struggle and failure happen for students (and ourselves as educators), it is how we interpret these experiences that determines how we feel about ourselves as learners (Barron, 2022; Kolb & Kolb, 2009). How teachers communicate the meaning of setbacks, struggle, and failure is critical to students' mindsets. This builds self-management, one of the five CASEL social-emotional competencies, as discussed in the introduction. Educators can express genuine interest in student thinking while setting and modeling clear norms for how the class will respond to mistakes and see them as learning opportunities.

Nurturing this mindset to have our students believe they can succeed also helps them overcome some negative self-images they possess due to their lived experiences outside of school. It's easier to believe in "can't" when a lack of opportunity or experience has been a part of your world. Educational consultant Brian Butler talks about the opportunity gap that exists for many of our students, and he frames it by imagining each student's lived experiences resulting in them having more cups to turn over and explore as opportunities (personal communication, 2023). Students who are supported at home, taken to activities, read to, and encouraged to explore in their first five years might arrive with one hundred cups. He suggests each cup turned over represents an opportunity, and he contrasts that with a student who has significantly fewer opportunities and might arrive with four cups. To make matters worse, those four cups might be turned over and yield no future interests for the students and lead them to, at a very early age, believing that success is not a viable outcome. School becomes a thirteen-year sentence, rather than thirteen years of exploration and opportunity to develop and hone strengths.

Measure Progress and Success in This Mindset

Measuring progress and celebrating when students make progress in relation to reasonable expectations is an effective way of nurturing this mindset. While it may seem like a straightforward extension that adopting the mindset of "I can succeed at this" would lead to improved outcomes, it is important both to validate this through research and practice and to identify some strategies or examples that amplify the desired outcome. A body of research suggests that educators who incorporate this academic mindset and the behaviors that support it see improved results, particularly for low-achieving students. Snipes and Alexander Jacobson (2021) revealed that:

Even after individual differences in prior achievement were controlled for, differences in grade 5 measures of growth mindset, performance avoidance, and academic behaviors were related (as a group) to significant differences in how well students navigated the transition to middle school. These relationships seemed to be meaningful among lower-achieving grade 5 students and appeared to be largest among the lowest-achieving students. (p. 13)

Lisa B. Limeri and colleagues (2020) further suggest that academic performance influences students' mindsets. Their research implies that "mindset and academic performance constitute a positive feedback loop." In other words, performance is spawned by the positive mindset of "I can succeed at this," which, when cultivated, produces better performance. The authors outlined "five factors that students reported as influencing their mindset beliefs: academic experiences, observing peers, deducing logically, taking societal cues, and formal learning." How might educators incorporate opportunities to further these factors in their classrooms? Here are a few suggestions.

Have Students Set Goals and Reflect on Them

The next time your students each set a goal around achieving a particular outcome, have them reflect on their journey toward meeting the goal, and—regardless of their success—ask them to identify what they learned through the process of striving to achieve the goal. Dan Wolf is the literacy coordinator in Woodridge School District 68 in Woodridge, Illinois. He supports colleagues through the creation of a monthly calendar of SEL activities that educators use in their classrooms on each day of the month. Figure 2.1 (page 48) is an example of this monthly calendar, and you can read more about student goal setting on page 67.

You can see the following ideas boldfaced in the calendar.

- **Goal setting:** This feature appears at the start and end of the month. On the first, students each set a goal for the month. This goal is determined by the student. Halfway through the month, students review their progress toward the goal. At the end of the month, the student reflects on the goal and how and why they did or did not achieve their goal. Have students contemplate the following questions.
    - What did you do that helped you to achieve that result?
    - How much time did you spend achieving the outcome?

Monday	Tuesday	Wednesday	Thursday	Friday
Have students write a **goal** for themselves for this month and the steps they should take to accomplish it.	Start **gratitude journals** with your students.	Have your students practice yoga doing all or part of the video "Yoga for Kids!" (Storyhive, 2017) at http://tinyurl.com/5fezmtsb.	Practice **box breathing** as a mindfulness tool.	Read and discuss *Namaste Is a Greeting* by Suma Subramaniam and Sandhya Prabhat (2022).
Have students write a letter introducing themselves to their teacher for next year. What do they want their teacher to know?	Write each student's name on a slip of paper; put all students' names in a bag; have every student choose one slip and state a positive quality of the person whose name they drew.	Complete the **five senses exercise**.	Read and discuss *A World of Plausibilities: An Exercise in Mindfulness* by Frank J. Sileo and Jennifer Zivoin (2017).	Give students back the **goals** they set for themselves and have them reflect on their progress so far.
Read and discuss *What I'm Feeling Is Okay!* by Laura Shiff and Bev Johnson (2021).	Try the mindfulness exercise **balanced breathing.**	Have students write a letter or make a card as an act of gratitude for a staff member in the building, thanking them for all they do.	Take one last class photo.	Have students create a video message encouraging themselves to do their best next year. Students can save these to their Google Drive to watch at the beginning of next school year.
Eat lunch with your class one last time.	Read and discuss *The Year We Learned to Fly* by Jacqueline Woodson and Rafael López (2022).	Practice **balloon belly breathing** with students.	Have your students look over and read everything they wrote in their **gratitude journals**.	Return students' **goals** to them; have them reflect on whether they met their goal and what their next steps should be.

Source: © 2024 by Dan Wolf. Used with permission.

Figure 2.1: SEL calendar.

- What strategy did you use to help you achieve your goal?

While achieving the goal may seem more directly aligned with the mindset of this chapter, understanding the learning that occurs as goals are achieved is essential to developing the belief that makes this mindset attainable.

- **Gratitude journals:** After you buy a car, have you ever suddenly noticed how everyone drives the same car you have? How about when you're having a bad day and *everything* that day goes wrong? When you focus on a particular thing, it can completely shift your mindset. Use it to your advantage! Writing a gratitude journal or list with your students will help them begin to focus more on the positive. Not only does gratitude work to improve one's perspective, but it can increase inclusivity because "gratitude is one avenue to encourage prosocial behavior" (Del Castillo, 2022). That, in turn, can also positively affect the "I belong in this academic community" mindset (page 9). Students can get creative and decorate the journal cover or the page. Take a few minutes every day to have the student record some things they are grateful for or that went well. See the reproducible "Gratitude Journal Prompts" (page 27) for prompts you can use.

- **Box breathing:** See the reproducible "Mindfulness Exercises" (page 52) for instructions for these and other listed breathing exercises.
  - Five senses exercise
  - Balanced breathing
  - Balloon belly breathing

If designing a monthlong calendar feels like too much, incorporate minilessons several times a week to launch the lesson and set the intention of practicing positive mindsets throughout the lesson, day, week, and month. Again, refer to figure 2.1 for an example and use the reproducible "Mindset Minilesson Design" (page 20).

Reframe Failure

Reframe your failures as learning opportunities. Refer to the "Frame Mistakes and Struggle as Normal and Productive" section of chapter 2 (page 45) for how educators can assist students to process failure by helping them set and review their goals. Model this for your students by sharing a time when you didn't achieve the outcome you set out to achieve.

- What were your expectations about success going into the event or challenge?
- How did you fail?
- What did you learn from this failure?
- What were the skills or learnings you gained while working toward achieving the goal?

The COVID-19 pandemic may serve as a great example as educators were challenged in unprecedented ways and had to learn new skills, sometimes through a trial-and-error process.

Break It Up

This strategy often reminds us of the formidable challenge presented when asked how one might eat an elephant. The whimsical answer of *one bite at a time* is apropos for this strategy. Do your students find the thought of a difficult task daunting? Guide them to set small but achievable tasks and goals and break the large task down into smaller, more manageable chunks. If they need more knowledge or information before they start the task, then have them set that as their first goal. For example, an elementary student might have trouble remembering all the facets of a story, but they might recall some random chunks. Have that student share the chunks and work with them on sequencing to build their response. A secondary student might not know how to completely solve a mathematical problem but perhaps has an entry point, part of a solution, or some general mathematical knowledge. Taking these pieces and having them work with another student might help to frame a more complete response.

Action Items

This chapter has focused on the need for our students (and ourselves) to adopt a mindset of positive capacity and outcomes. "I can succeed at this" involves components of belief, productive struggle, striving for growth, and faith in the notion of *yet* as an indication that growth is possible. This is a mindset foundational to this book and a lynchpin for the other mindsets. Having reflected on the importance of students being able to positively say, "I can succeed at this," consider which of the following action items you can tackle individually or with your colleagues to nurture this mindset broadly.

- Review the suggestions within the chapter in comparison to what your school and district are already doing so that you can possibly weave next steps into existing initiatives and commitments.

- Spend time during collaborative team time, staff meetings, and professional learning to determine ways that teachers, grade levels, curricular departments, and the school can help students truly believe they can be successful with tasks, with school, and with life. Linking success to interest may help students push through a challenge (Harackiewicz, Smith, & Priniski, 2016).

- Model and promote the belief that all staff and students are capable of growth, and that when growth and progress are achieved, through focus and effort, success is inevitable.

- Design learning experiences that are accessible to all students and organize the learning so that all students have confidence they can complete the assignment or assessment without becoming discouraged.

- Challenge all students to make progress and achieve. Nurturing the mindset of "I can succeed at this" does not mean presenting students who are not at proficiency yet with watered-down tasks and expectations. These students will interpret this negatively, as giving up on them. Instead, for all students, please consider adopting our definition of *rigor*: that place just beyond where a student currently resides. Then, assign tasks to students that push them just beyond.

- Engage in professional learning—this book and its resource guides may help your efforts.

The reproducible "'I Can Succeed at This' Action Plan" (page 54) helps teams hold collaborative conversations, guided by this action plan, to reflect on where they are and identify next steps they can take.

Mindfulness Exercises

These are different breathing exercises that can help improve your mindfulness. You can close your eyes while you do the breathing exercises, or simply look down, to help focus.

Box Breathing

Box breathing focuses on counts of four, like the sides of a box.

1. Breathe in slowly through your nose as you silently count to four. Focus on feeling the air go into your lungs.
2. Hold your breath and silently count to four.
3. Slowly breathe out, through your mouth, and silently count to four.
4. Hold and silently count to four.
5. Repeat until you feel calmer.

Balanced Breathing

Balanced breathing focuses on breathing from your diaphragm. Throughout the exercise, your right hand—on your chest—should not move up and down as you inhale and exhale. If it does, use your diaphragm (or "stomach") instead. When you do that, you'll notice your stomach moving as you inhale and exhale.

1. Sit tall, with your spine straight, but not rigid. Your chin should be parallel to the floor.
2. Put your left hand on your stomach, and your right hand on your chest.
3. Breathe in slowly through your nose and silently count to four. Notice your left hand and belly go up.
4. Slowly breathe out, through your mouth, and silently count to four. Notice your left hand and belly go down.
5. Do this three or four times. If you practice consistently, go up to ten breaths.

Balloon Belly Breathing

Balloon belly breathing focuses on feeling, internally and externally, the sensation of your stomach moving as you breathe.

1. Put your hands on your stomach.
2. Breathe slowly in through your nose. Feel your stomach expand like it is an inflating balloon.
3. Count silently to four.
4. Slowly breathe out through your mouth for four seconds. Feel your stomach deflate, like a balloon with the air let out.
5. Repeat until you feel calmer.

Positive Behaviors Start With Positive Mindsets © 2024 Solution Tree Press • SolutionTree.com
Visit **go.SolutionTree.com/behavior** to download this free reproducible.

Five Senses

This exercise requires you to draw your attention away from your emotions and notice your surroundings and name them.

1. Name five things you can see.
2. Name four things you can feel.
3. Name three things you can hear.
4. Name two things you can smell.
5. Name one thing you can taste.

"I Can Succeed at This" Action Plan

Among your collaborative teams, discuss these issues and create plans to address the ideas and suggestions recommended in this chapter.

Possible Action Area	Progress-Monitoring Suggestion	Next Steps
Set High Expectations In what ways can staff explicitly establish and communicate high achievement expectations for all students, to students and parents?	In leadership and in collaborative teams, document expectations for mindsets and behaviors; use surveys as well as numbers and types of behavioral incidents to measure positive progress.	
Allow Voice and Choice In what ways can students be given opportunities to shape the elements of assignments and assessments? In what ways can students be given choices in regard to which portions of assignments and assessments they complete?	Select a strategy mentioned in this chapter and measure the impact on your classroom culture and overall learning.	

Possible Action Area	Progress-Monitoring Suggestion	Next Steps
Give Specific Feedback How can the feedback given to students on their work be even more specific and positive?	Identify small chunks of the learning outcomes and commit to offering specific, growth-oriented feedback to students that focuses on one or two mindsets or skills; always pair the feedback with a positive attribute about the student's work.	
Adopt a Growth Mindset How can instruction and assessment be crafted to promote a growth mindset (see chapter 4, page 79) so that students believe they can succeed?	Choose an assignment or activity where the only feedback offered is written/verbal and speaks to adding to the responses rather than evaluating them.	

Possible Action Area	Progress-Monitoring Suggestion	Next Steps
Make Expectations Clear, Realistic, and Reasonable What steps can staff take to make the next goal toward proficiency seem doable?	Review all the assessment items currently in use to ensure clarity. For example, if you are looking for three pieces of evidence, make sure the question asks for that.	
Set Goals What steps can staff take to make short-term goal setting toward longer-term goals a regular part of teaching and learning?	Discuss and decide on long-term and short-term goals; determine how you will know you have reached the goal and how you will celebrate; focus on your next, first steps toward the goals.	

Possible Action Area	Progress-Monitoring Suggestion	Next Steps
Establish a Culture of Progress In what ways can student progress (and not simply achievement) be measured, communicated, and celebrated?	Discuss your norms for sharing evidence and determine if you are acknowledging growth or only achievement; consider whether to use data walls or other tracking to ensure and show growth toward proficiency.	
Scaffold and Differentiate How can curriculum, instruction, and assessment be scaffolded and differentiated to ensure that students can access learning and so that their current levels of learning can be most accurately measured?	Decide whether your evidence-gathering tools help your teams either plan ways to ensure all students learn and grow or make excuses by providing remediation and labeling with an eye toward a designation rather than believing all students can learn.	

Learning Targets

By the end of this chapter, you'll be able to reflect positively on the following statements.

- I can identify and employ strategies and actions to ensure that students believe school and the experiences within the school have a purpose and relevance.

- I can create environments and activities within which all students feel that school and school activities have a value to their lives.

CHAPTER 3

"This Work Has Value for Me"

We have often encountered students who, frustratedly, express the sentiment, "Why am I learning this stuff?" Educational consultant Jeremy S. Greenfield (2022) explains that if students see the value and connection in their learning and this is paired with a belief that they have the competence to succeed, they tend to show greater motivation, greater perseverance, and more effective study strategies. As suggested in the opening sentence, this is not a new struggle; the late educational researcher Phillip C. Schlechty (1997) summed it up this way:

> The business of schools is to produce work that . . . is so compelling that students persist when they experience difficulties, and that is so challenging that students have a sense of accomplishment, of satisfaction—indeed, of delight—when they successfully accomplish the tasks assigned. (p. 58)

This means that as educators, from the first day of class forward, we must explicitly clarify the what, why, and how of school to students' present and future lives.

"This work has value for me" is a mindset that is equally important in the behavioral domain as it is in ensuring that students master academic targets. So let's dive into the meaning of this mindset, the why for students' adopting it, and the means by which we can nurture this mindset among students to ensure their success in the classroom and beyond.

What Does "This Work Has Value for Me" Mean?

"This work has value for me" means that students see the relevance and purpose in the assignments, activities, and experiences in the classroom, the school, and the broader educational community. It means that they see the connections of their education to their lives—not simply to their careers and avocations (sports, hobbies, and interests) but to their development as citizens and human beings. It means that they are permitted and required to have agency—they play an active role in their learning. Through this agency, they are more likely to see the value, purpose, relevance, and meaning of school because they are involved, they are responsible, and it's personal (Brophy, 2008; Goodman & Eren, 2013; Vaughn, 2018). Explicitly connecting learning and school to students' lives will go a long way toward nurturing motivated students. Dweck and colleagues (2014) state that when "non-cognitive factors are in place, students will look—and be—motivated. In fact, these non-cognitive factors constitute what psychological researchers call *motivation*, and fostering these mindsets and self-regulation strategies is what psychological researchers typically mean by *motivating* students" (p. 2). Fostering mindsets such as ensuring that students see the value in school and schoolwork leads to more motivated students.

Students, particularly as they get older, often ask why they are completing a task and how the task relates to their lives now and in the future. As discussed in this chapter, while contextualizing tasks and experiences so that they connect to students' interests, passions, communities, and lives is important, it's not just about the nature of the task; it's also about the ways in which students are involved in the task. They have choice in the types of tasks or the ways in which they go about completing the task, and they have responsibilities in making sense of the task and in self-assessing and monitoring their evolving understanding (Greenfield, 2022). When students are more involved in the details and day-to-day tasks that make up school, they are more likely to see the relevance of school.

The value that students see in school and schoolwork is also enhanced when the work involves service to others or to ideas or causes that are important to their lives. In other words, the value perceived in school and schoolwork not only is improved when the experiences connect to their own personal goals but also impacts goals related to others aside from themselves (Bronk, 2012; Goodman & Eren, 2013).

It's not just about students knowing what they want to be when they grow up and tapping into that interest. Not all students are motivated, or solely motivated, by this goal, and of course, not all students know. Many students see value in relationships and in working with and supporting others; "this work has value for me" can be enhanced for these students when the completion of tasks is collaborative. Other students are motivated by connecting to and supporting their family and the community service-oriented aspects of experiences;

"this work has value for me" can be enhanced for these students by highlighting the benefit of school and learning experiences to their community and society at large (Goodman & Eren, 2013; Steger, Bundick, & Yeager, 2012). And of course, there are students who are simply motivated by always striving to do and be their best, which connects to and is enhanced by the fourth mindset, discussed in the next chapter.

Yes, each of these mindsets is complementary to the others. This third mindset is no different. For example, when students are more connected to their teachers, school, and broader school community—when they feel like they belong—they are more likely to see the value of school. And when students believe the work of school has value for them, they are more likely to feel connected to the content area, the classroom, and the school.

Why Focus on "This Work Has Value for Me"?

Research clearly validates the notion that student behaviors and academic success are positively impacted when the students believe that the work in which they are engaged and the experiences they have in school have value, purpose, and relevance (Bronk, 2012; Hill, Burrow, & Sumner, 2013). We are the answer we've been waiting for. If we are frustrated or dismayed or feel helpless when students communicate to us, verbally or otherwise, that they do not see the purpose of school, then taking action—doing something about it—just makes sense. The research confirms that taking steps that help students see value in school pays off.

When students see purpose and relevance in school, in the content areas they study, and in the work with which they are asked to engage, they are more likely to possess a positive mindset and more likely to be successful in school (Bronk, 2012; Brophy, 2008; Hill et al., 2013; Yeager, Bundick, & Johnson, 2012). This applies to adults as well; when we believe there is value in what we are doing, we have a more positive mindset. And when we have a more positive mindset, we experience more success in school and in life.

The degree to which students value an academic task strongly influences their persistence and performance at the task (Duckworth & Carlson, 2013; Goodman & Eren, 2013; Steger et al., 2012; Vaughn, 2018). That persistence and performance are directly tied to any given work making sense to students and being something they can link to experiences in their lives.

Students are motivated to learn, and they display positive mindsets, when the tasks they are assigned are interesting to them and they believe that the tasks are related to their lives (Brophy, 2008; Steger, 2012; Vaughn, 2020; Yeager et al., 2012). Moreover, when students are involved in the creation, design, and monitoring of the task, their mindsets lead to greater levels of motivation.

When students have interest in a content area or subject area and believe that there is a connection between content areas or subjects and their future goals, students are more likely to persist, demonstrate consistent effort, and display the learning strategies and academic behaviors that lead to school success (Brophy, 2008; Hill et al., 2013; Walton & Cohen, 2011; Yeager et al., 2012). Goal setting and agency, as discussed later in the chapter, enhance the value that students see in school and improve their mindsets.

A final rationale for focusing on this mindset: The state of California recently approved a new framework for mathematics that is aligned with current research on mindsets. The framework of the California Department of Education (2023) states:

> Students who use mathematics powerfully can maintain this connection between mathematical ideas and the relevance of these ideas to meaningful contexts. At some point between the primary grades and high school graduation, however, too many students lose that sense of connection. They are left wondering, what does this have to do with me or my experiences? Why do I need to know this? Absent tasks or projects that enable them to experience that connection and purpose, they end up seeing mathematics as an exercise in memorized procedures that match different problem types.

To that end, educators are encouraged to connect "drivers of investigation" ("make sense of the world," "predict what could happen," "impact the future") to mathematical big ideas, content standards, and practices. Why? Because, as the framework states, students "actively engage in learning when they find purpose and meaning in the learning" (California Department of Education, 2023). It's clear: the relevance of learning to students makes a significant difference in mindsets, motivation, and learning.

While we are introducing the third of the four mindsets described in this book, let us note that readers are likely seeing overlaps and interconnections; they definitely exist. In the context of developing this chapter's mindset, we find that students' sense of belonging contributes to their seeing more purpose and relevance. When students see more value in school, we see them being more likely to feel a greater sense of belonging. Plus, we see that when students feel they can be successful with a task, they are likely to find more value in the task; likewise, when work makes sense to students and they believe there is a purpose and payoff, they may be more likely to begin the work with a greater belief in their ability to succeed.

The question, then, is, How do we make school, schoolwork, and the broader school experience relevant and of interest to all students? While a tall task indeed, there are practical steps we can take to ensure that students see value in the work.

How Do We Nurture Students' Sense That "This Work Has Value for Me"?

As with the other mindsets, nurturing students' belief that the work, the content area, the classroom, and the school have value, purpose, and relevance for them will be positively impacted by the adults on campus taking steps to ensure the tasks and the ways in which students experience and complete the tasks connect to their lives, interests, cultures, and communities and when we actively involve them in their learning. Allowing student voice and choice (page 42) is one way to nurture it.

What follows are additional practical, proven ideas that work: involving students in the creation of school and classroom norms, visions, missions, and compacts; ensuring teaching and learning that showcase the value of learning a topic or skill; facilitating meaningful goal setting; promoting agency; employing learning target trackers; customizing curriculum, instruction, and assessment; and paving the way for extracurricular activities.

Cocreate School and Classroom Norms, Visions, Missions, and Compacts

Actively and authentically involve students in creating the school and classroom norms, as well as vision, mission, and compact (collective commitments). At elementary and secondary schools, engage the student council or a more representative group of students in providing the detailed expectations aligned to the school's vision. Have these groups record videos of students exhibiting positive behaviors. Students are more likely to buy into these statements and commitments and strive to meet the expectations articulated in them when they are invited to be coauthors and codevelopers.

Moreover, ask them to assess their own success in meeting these commitments and the success of their class and the school. The surveys in this book (pages 26 and 90) are one way students can self-assess their ability to meet expectations. Consider adding mindset and behavioral targets, based on cocreated commitments, to learning target trackers (page 69) and ask students to self-assess. In addition to students monitoring their academic outcomes, adding mindset or other behavioral learning targets to trackers is an excellent way of increasing the status and importance of mindsets. That addition is also a way to avoid needing another tool or a separate time for students to assess their mindsets and behaviors.

As you implement the described strategies and seek and review these data, remember that schools are communities of their own. When students directly contribute to the rules, they see the part they play in their classrooms, school family, and broader community. Another way of increasing the extent to which students see the relevance of school at any level is to invite former students to visit the school or classrooms to talk about their learning journey and perhaps the importance of positive mindsets (Dalakas, 2016; Robinson, 2018). Have high schoolers visit elementary and middle schoolers; have college students or those in the workforce visit the middle and high schoolers. Reach out to colleagues, families, local professional organizations, high schools, and colleges to identify potential guest speakers and then prepare your students for active engagement (through a graphic organizer to take notes). Then, actively facilitate the guest speaking session.

Invite students' active and authentic participation in defining the school- and classroom-level expectations and operations concerning behaviors and the ways that the "business" of school is conducted (Alter & Haydon, 2017; Bennett, 2014). When students have a voice in these important decisions, they feel more connected to school and invested in, and committed to, the agreements that the school hopes and expects all students will enthusiastically meet (Fuligni, 2019). Work toward this goal with the following strategies.

- **Select students (or have students select peers) to participate in behavior or PBIS committees that are tasked with determining behavioral priorities and the ways these priorities are met:** These students can come from one or multiple existing student groups, or staff or students can nominate a few students per grade level to meet before the school year begins (or during the first few opening days) to review existing schoolwide norms and expectations and make suggestions for improvements. The group provides detailed examples of what meeting these expectations looks and sounds like and can, as noted earlier, record videos of someone meeting those expectations. Many schools' behavioral expectations do not yet represent the mindsets described in this book, so task this group with ensuring that the four mindsets are included. Once created, schedule time for staff and students to share the expectations class by class or at a schoolwide assembly.

- **Engage all students in a given class or period in cocreating classroom commitments:** Perhaps building on the schoolwide norms described in the preceding bullet, spend time in each class or period hearing from all student voices to more concretely list, define, and describe how students ideally behave and engage in a specific grade, class, or course and how the class will positively and productively learn. We recommend that the teacher first facilitate a brainstorm of all contributions, and then, with students, categorize and organize the class consensus before writing the final list of norms and expectations on chart paper. Finally, ask each member of the classroom community to sign and commit to the expectations represented. Revisit these classroom expectations often, possibly during classroom meetings, to ensure that students recall the standards that they created and to which they have committed, and to highlight specific norms that require more attention at various points of the year.

- **Ask teachers to nominate students representing various student groups and levels of academic and social-behavioral success to meet with educator leaders to provide feedback on what is going well, and not going as well, at the school:** Using either the same group of students involved in creating the schoolwide set of norms and expectations or a new representative group, meet regularly with students to hear from them about the success of students in the school in meeting the agreed-on standards for mindsets and behaviors; solicit input on what the school can do to make necessary adjustments. Students will be, and feel, heard, and staff will benefit from student-level feedback on what is and is not yet working in terms of positive and productive student behaviors.

The idea is that students feel as though they belong because they have been asked to participate in, and are authentically involved in, the determination of what the classroom and school stands for—the way things are done in the classroom or school.

Providing examples of what students in previous classes experienced and what they did to be successful speaks to the possibilities for all students. Teachers should also promote behavioral norms such as maintaining regular attendance, engaging in active note-taking, taking part in class activities, and asking questions. It is essential for teachers to establish desired norms and habits on the very first day. For example, consider an activity on the first day that establishes the norm of students talking to one another and participating in class discussions, and possibly discussing how collaborating and communicating with others is a life skill—one that they will learn and practice in school, every day. If the teacher doesn't explicitly establish this norm, then the status quo of the usual talkers participating will persist, while other students will unfortunately embrace the norm of staying quiet; those students who are quiet are likely to question the value and relevance of school to them.

Explain Why They Are Learning a Topic or Skill

Consistently—each day and at the beginning of a new lesson or learning experience—connect the content and concepts, skills, and learning processes to students' present and future lives. For example, at the elementary level, you may connect the importance of literacy or numeracy to students' lives. As important and relevant, connect the importance of listening, speaking, and working with others—tasks that occur throughout every elementary school day—to the rest of students' school careers. For secondary students, connections between academic concepts and students' futures may be clear to students, particularly when their college and career goals match the content area. Even when they do not match explicitly, connect the process skills in your course and their academic standards (such as the Standards for Mathematical Practice, the Science and Engineering Practices, the Historical and Social Sciences Analysis Skills) to the ways people learn and complete tasks in any workplace (or, for example, when managing finances or health care in their personal lives as adults). The answer to the question "Why am I learning this?" may not only relate to a specific academic standard (such as solving systems of linear equations); a significant part of the answer may relate to *how* they are learning (for example, by problem solving in a collaborative group).

Over time, ask students to provide the answer. As staff consistently model for students why the what and the how of learning are connected to their lives, students should be able to, and should assume responsibilities for, providing answers to these questions. Several times a week, ask students to orally or in writing respond to this question as part of their exit slips. Posing and answering this question not only provides a rationale for the relevance of school and schoolwork, but it also demonstrates the importance of the question itself—it makes it OK to ask the question and in fact communicates to students that we should be asking the question. Research supports the idea that students' emotional responses to learning impacts their engagement level and the extent to which they learn, and student ownership of the learning purpose is key to a positive emotional response (Aldous, 2014; Immordino-Yang & Faeth, 2010). Showing students the value of what they're learning can also mean not only explaining it in simple terms outright, but mixing things up in instruction. Use simple or more complex gamification elements. There are many game-based learning platforms; you can create a book or classroom scavenger hunt (for finding answers that match questions in a book or around the classroom) or create learning breakouts (or many other gamified experiences) with the Google Workspace. In addition, celebrate and give status to practice standards, not just content standards, by highlighting their importance and giving feedback and assessing student progress and performance on them (for example, Standards for Mathematical Practice, Science and Engineering Practices, Historical and Social Sciences Analysis Skills); these practice standards may be viewed by students as more relevant to their lives than content standards.

Help Set Classroom Goals and Connect Them to a Purpose for Learning

Regularly ask students to set short- and long-term goals and connect classroom and school experiences to these goals. For example, during morning meetings at elementary and secondary schools, ask students to record the short- and long-term goals to which they are committed. Later, these same classroom meeting times are opportunities for students to reflect on why they have or have not yet met their goals and discuss with a partner or the class what their next steps are; how will they make adjustments to meet the goal, or what will they do to continue meeting the goal? Table 3.1 (page 68) offers examples of short- and long-term goals for elementary and secondary students.

Connect the purpose for learning to both students' self-interest *and* their self-transcendent goals (for example, *I want to be a doctor because it would be enjoyable and financially rewarding* and *would help people*).

Table 3.1: Short- and Long-Term Goals for Elementary and Secondary Students

Elementary Students	
Examples of *short-term goals*:	Examples of *long-term goals*:
Completing all classwork on time	Becoming an excellent writer
Developing and following a morning and after-school routine	Making the high school sports team, music ensemble, or play
Learning to draw a favorite character	Developing and maintaining lifelong healthy habits
Learning a piece of music	
Practicing a new move in their favorite sport	
Secondary Students	
Examples of *short-term goals*:	Examples of *long-term goals*:
Completing all assignments in time to receive feedback prior to submitting the work for final assessment	Learning another language
	Traveling to another state, province, or country
Applying for admittance to an organization	Getting into college or trade school
Earning an improved grade point average	Creating and following a career plan
Trying a new sport or activity	

Dedicating time for students to think about their goals is important in its own right; they may not know what their goals are, or they might not have defined their aspirations with clarity and details. Goal setting will also help students see that school is directly and indirectly connected to their goals, particularly if we help them make these explicit connections. Remind students that there is a big world in which they exist, and it is waiting for them to embrace it. Each experience in which they engage in school is either directly or indirectly preparing them for that world and for meeting their goals. Set similar goals for yourself, whether they apply to your personal or professional life. Take the same steps that you're asking students to take, and talk about your progress with them so the students can see that learning lasts a lifetime; you're modeling growth.

To further enhance the purpose, relevance, and value that students see, explain the connection between their active involvement in defining and describing the school's and classroom's rules and expectations and their monitoring toward those expectations—to goal setting. Have students set goals regarding how successfully individuals, the class, or the school are meeting mindset and behavioral expectations and model the process by setting a goal yourself. For example, if positive, appropriate language is a goal, students set goals around their *own* language, and administrators set a schoolwide goal of one week without any notice of hurtful, hateful, negative, or profane language. Make setting short- and long-term goals part of your classroom and school culture; it is a worthwhile, research-based practice (Martin et al., 2022).

Encourage Agency

Student voice and *agency* are similar, but briefly describing the differences can help collaborative teams ensure that they are providing opportunities for students to exercise both their voice and agency. As noted in this chapter, students see school as more relevant (and have a greater sense of belonging) when their voice is included in determining and defining the rules and expectations; promoting student *voice* means actively soliciting student input on meaningful aspects of the school and classroom and incorporating their voice into policies and practices. We promote student *agency* when we invite or require students to take more ownership and responsibility for their learning (Pearson, 2023).

Just as students are provided with voice and choice, require them to take responsibility for the efficient, safe, and productive operation of their environment, and for the completion of their assignments. When students have a stake in their learning, they are likely to have agency. Promote this agency by assigning them tasks, jobs, and responsibilities. For example, assign students, on a rotating basis, the responsibility of keeping class on track with the elements of the lesson or the day's schedule, or assign students the responsibility for supplies and materials. Assign *all* students the responsibility of recording the lesson's objectives or learning targets and require *all* students to reflect upon their levels of understanding of the lesson. As with voice and choice, when students play an active role in school experiences, they will see school as an integral part of their lives. One way of promoting agency and providing opportunities for students to experience the relevance of school to their lives is through the use of learning target trackers.

Use Learning Target Trackers

Trackers are introduced to students before a unit of instruction begins so they know the expectations for their upcoming learning. As a unit proceeds, students record their evolving level of understanding based on their own self-assessment of their proficiency and based on feedback they receive from their teacher on formative assessments. When there are opportunities for Tier 2 response to intervention supports, students and teachers know the targets that warrant reteaching and supports. Following the summative assessment, students and teachers can see the standards on which they need additional instruction and practice prior to completing a reassessment.

Learning Target Description	Attempt One	Attempt Two	Attempt Three	Overall
I can identify linear and nonlinear relationships from a table.	4			4
I can identify linear and nonlinear relationships from a graph.	1	2	3	3
I can identify linear and nonlinear relationships from an equation.	2	2	3	3
I can identify proportional and nonproportional relationships from a table.	3	4	3	4
I can identify proportional and nonproportional relationships from a graph.	1	1	2	2

Mastery Level

- I am starting to get it — 20%
- I got it — 40%
- I almost got it — 40%

Source: © 2024 by Irvine Unified School District, Irvine, California. Used with permission.
Source for standards: National Governors Association Center for Best Practices & Council of Chief State School Officers, 2010.

Figure 3.1: Example learning target tracker.

Learning target trackers like the one in figure 3.1 can help students see the value of their learning journey since they are expressing agency for their progress. When students have not yet met a target, they are empowered to self-advocate and ask for assistance with a specific learning goal.

Mastery Level	Error Type Attempt One	Error Type Attempt Two	Error Type Attempt Three
I got it	No Error	No Error	No Error
I almost got it	Careless Error	Computational Error	Careless Error
I almost got it	Conceptual Error	Computational Error	Careless Error
I got it	Computational Error	No Error	Careless Error
I'm starting to get it	Conceptual Error	Conceptual Error	Conceptual Error

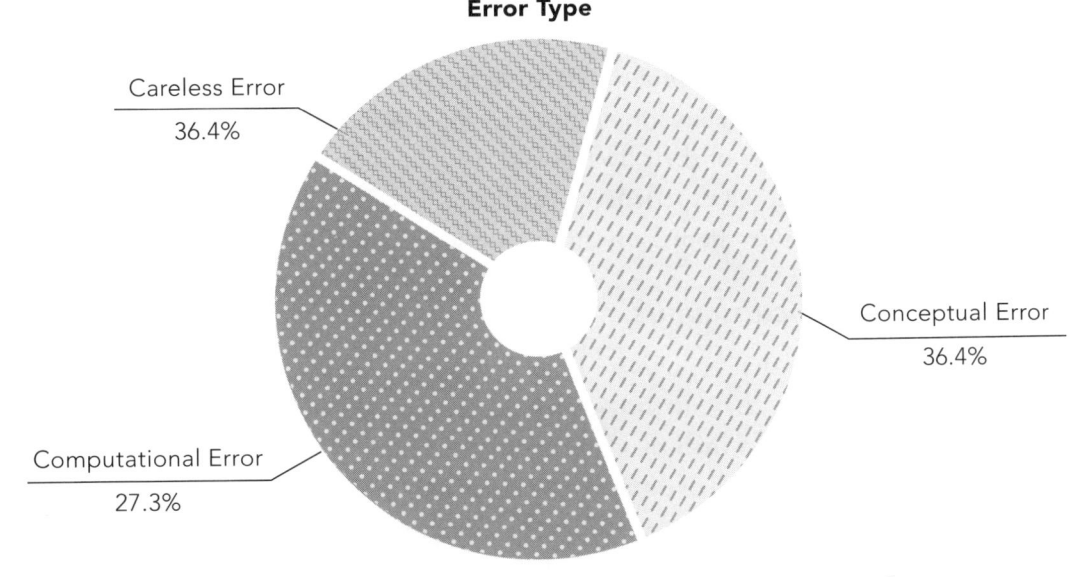

To have students use learning target trackers, follow these steps.

1. Start by establishing the purpose of learning by determining academic and behavioral learning targets and sharing them with students often, at the beginning of and throughout the unit or learning experiences that relate to the targets.

2. Then, give frequent, formative feedback to students on these targets and have students record their evolving progress on a tracking form.

3. Finally, have students self-assess where they believe they are now in relation to mastering targets and ask them to reflect on the why behind their current levels of understanding and what they need to continue to make progress.

When students are actively involved in tracking their progress, they are much more likely to see the value in school. Learning target trackers also help students see that their ability and competence grow with effort, the mindset addressed in chapter 4 (page 79).

Customize Curriculum, Instruction, and Assessment

Whenever possible, use the information that you have learned about students and their interests to customize your assignments and assessments. This could be as simple as using student names and hobbies in problems or tasks or developing tasks that relate to students' lives (for example, encouraging students to write their opinion paper on their favorite internet personality or having them complete a perimeter-and-area project related to their favorite outdoor hobby). This certainly takes time, so start simple and start small. When students literally see themselves and aspects of their lives outside of school in schoolwork, they are likely to see value in the experiences in which they are engaged and feel as though they belong in the school community, as discussed in chapter 1 (page 9).

Encourage Extracurriculars

Take steps to ensure that students are interested and see value in the extracurricular opportunities that are provided. Survey students to ask the type of extracurricular activity in which they are most interested and require that students participate in some form of extracurricular (for example, science fair, sports, music). Extracurriculars are *extra* by definition. However, given the throughline that students viewing school as more relevant, purposeful, and valuable leads to more positive mindsets, which leads to more positive behaviors and higher levels of academic achievement, and extracurriculars can help boost those views (Im, Hughes, Cao, & Kwok, 2016), reframing extracurriculars as required is a worthwhile goal. If no extracurricular activities match a student interest identified in the survey, work with staff to offer such an activity. A sample survey was provided in chapter 1 (page 22).

As an example, one middle school we work with created a weekly schedule that embeds time for an additional once-weekly elective. Each teacher offers a class (chess, crochet, movie critique, ultimate Frisbee) for which students have a passion; students select their first, second, and third choices. For a trimester, students engage in a favored experience that is also a keen interest of one of the school's teachers. When students are connected to more aspects of school (sometimes beyond academics) and to their educators, they see increased value and relevance in school to their lives.

Action Items

This chapter identified strategies and actions that lead to students believing that school and the experiences in it have a purpose and relevance; the chapter also helps educators shape their environments and activities so all students feel that school and school activities have value. When students see that value, relevance, and purpose in their school experiences, they are more likely to have a positive mindset. That mindset leads to better social skills, more perseverance, better use of learning strategies, more productive academic behaviors, and higher levels of academic achievement.

Having reflected on the importance of students being able to positively say, "This work has value for me," consider which of the following action items you can tackle individually or with your colleagues to nurture this mindset broadly.

- Review the suggestions within the chapter in comparison to what your school and district are already doing so that you can possibly weave next steps into existing initiatives and commitments.

- Spend time during collaborative team time, staff meetings, and professional learning to determine ways that assignments, assessments, and learning experiences can be more relevant and connected to students' lives.

- Engage in conversations that speak to the relevance of the learning at hand. The response to the age-old question "Why am I learning this stuff?" has to generate a better response than "Because I said so,"

"It's in the curriculum," or some artificial global impact. In addition to their sense of self, students learn about and understand their place in society, fostering a sense of belonging and acceptance in both their school community and the community at large. If teachers use engaging, purposeful teaching materials, it will help all students succeed while also cultivating their desire for lifelong learning.

- Inventory the ways that students can connect to school beyond academics (arts, music, sports, clubs, other extracurricular options) and survey student interests—match current options to student interests and work toward offering options that meet student interests but are not yet available.

- Engage in professional learning—this book and its resource guides may help your efforts.

The reproducible "'This Work Has Value for Me' Action Plan" helps teams hold collaborative conversations, guided by this action plan, to reflect on where they are and identify next steps they can take.

"This Work Has Value for Me" Action Plan

Among your collaborative teams, discuss these issues and create plans to address the ideas and suggestions recommended in this chapter.

Possible Action Area	Progress-Monitoring Suggestion	Next Steps
Cocreate School and Classroom Agreements How can students be authentically involved in shaping the ideals and expectations that directly influence the culture, climate, and behaviors in classrooms and schoolwide?	Using the surveys in this book or those created by your collaborative teams, ask students to assess the extent they have been authentically involved in shaping school and classroom expectations.	
Explain Why Students Are Learning Something In what ways can staff devote time to setting a purpose for the content and processes of learning and involve students in connecting experiences to their lives?	Regularly review student responses—on assignments and exit slips—where students have shared the ways topics and assignments relate to their lives.	
Set Goals In what ways can students be given opportunities to set goals about school assignments and activities that connect to their interests and aspirations and to impacts they can make in their broader communities?	Review student goals, give feedback on those goals, and ask students to measure the extent to which they are meeting or have met goals.	

page 1 of 2

Positive Behaviors Start With Positive Mindsets © 2024 Solution Tree Press • SolutionTree.com
Visit **go.SolutionTree.com/behavior** to download this free reproducible.

Possible Action Area	Progress-Monitoring Suggestion	Next Steps
Enable Agency How can students be given responsibilities within the school, in the classroom, and in the completion of academic work so that they understand that school has a relevance to their lives?	Document ways you are giving student responsibilities in classrooms; survey students regarding the amount of ownership and responsibility they feel in their learning.	
Use Learning Target Trackers What steps can staff take to communicate to students their progress toward learning specific learning targets, and how can students be directly involved in this tracking of progress?	Save and share the learning target trackers that measure, through grades, learning improvements that you can at least partly attribute to tracker use; survey the impact that students believe learning target trackers have on their mindsets and learning.	
Customize Curriculum, Instruction, and Assessment What steps can staff take to involve students' identities and interests in the work of the classroom?	Document ways teachers involve students' identities and interests in assignments; survey the extent to which student identities and interests are represented in class.	
Encourage Extracurricular Activities In what ways can the school ensure that students are connected to and involved in activities within the school and school community outside of academic coursework?	Gather and analyze data on student extracurricular involvement; use the data to increase both participation and engagement.	

Learning Targets

By the end of this chapter, you'll be able to reflect positively on the following statements.

- Every student is a success story waiting to be told.
- School is a thirteen-year experience, not thirteen ten-month experiences.
- Lifelong learning is the goal, not the option only available to some.
- Our beliefs determine our behaviors.

CHAPTER 4

"My Ability and Competence Grow With My Effort"

Most educators associate the mindset "My ability and competence grow with my effort" with the work of Carol S. Dweck, most notably in her groundbreaking book *Mindset: The New Psychology of Success* (Dweck, 2016). She describes a *growth mindset* as the belief that we can improve with effort and new strategies and that struggle is part of the process. This results in students believing they can practice and develop the academic, social, and emotional skills to stay motivated, set goals, and reflect on progress.

She contrasts this with a *fixed mindset*, where students (and often the adults who work with them) view struggle as a sign of inferiority and something to be avoided or disguised. In this fixed view, intelligence and success are not available to all students, and students who do not experience success quickly will likely adopt a belief that aligns with "I'm not good at this." More significantly, adults with fixed mindsets also believe that intelligence and success are beyond some students. It may get couched in positive speak about creating an opportunity ("If we could get Tommy any sort of employment in the adult world, it would be a win."), but the focal point is really about a predetermination that limits the potential of that student. Instead, the focus must remain on possibilities, not limitations.

We became educators not to chronicle what is but to make a difference in what could be. The current circumstances a student faces do not determine where the student ends up. They just determine the starting point. Educators help students plot the course. In that partnership, we see students grow in both ability and competence. This chapter discusses how to ensure that all students believe that their ability and competence can, and will, grow with effort. As in the preceding chapters, that is covered by considering the what, the why, and the how before introducing action items to tackle individually and with colleagues.

What Does "My Ability and Competence Grow With My Effort" Mean?

When students possess the mindset that their ability and competence will grow with their effort, they are in fact demonstrating that they've taken to heart two concepts essential to learning: (1) failure is not only necessary but desirable, and (2) lifelong learning is achievable and powerful. Educators fully embracing these beliefs is necessary before they can effectively communicate them to, and develop them in, students. It's equally important that educators model these concepts. Is it possible for you to not have all the answers or to potentially have a student know more about a topic than you do? Do educators model lifelong learning or just talk about it as a desired goal?

Understanding Failure as the Key to Rigor

For a long time, failure has been looked down on as a negative word or an even worse seven-letter *F*-word: *fatal*! It's therefore not surprising that the notion of failure is so stigmatized and has such a bad reputation. This has occurred at every level of education from grade school through university and has even crept into the world of work.

Although failure is seen as a worst-case scenario to be avoided at all costs, it doesn't have to be this way. Let's be clear—failure stings and can be uncomfortable and disheartening. It can stifle learning, but it's also a powerful learning tool. Failure can be a valuable companion in the learning cycle. While it is often viewed as the opposite of success, that dichotomy is a far too simplistic, narrow view. Success doesn't just happen, nor is it available to only a select few. It's often the final step in a long process of learning and growing with failure providing some guidance along the way. The prevailing negative view of failure doesn't have to exist—especially if we hope to cultivate in our students (and possibly rekindle in ourselves) the mindset that ability and competence grow with effort.

Perhaps the first step in rectifying this view of *failure* is to banish the word from our lexicon. Realistically, that is not going to happen, so a more prudent approach might begin with first trying to understand why it has negative connotations or, more importantly, why we value immediate success so highly. A study by researchers Robert C. Wilson, Amitai Shenhav, Mark Straccia, and Jonathan D. Cohen (2019) suggests that the pursuit of straight As (immediate success) may be the wrong goal. Their work suggests that learning is optimized when we fail approximately 15 percent of the time. Achieving only 85 percent of the time would not meet an A standard in most school settings! For those reading who think this is a familiar notion, you're likely familiar with the zone of proximal development, an idea first proposed by Lev Vygotsky (1997) in the 1930s. He described the sweet spot of learning as the stretch students might engage in when the learning is just beyond their current ability. Video game makers maximize this with the different levels they incorporate into their products that cause players to explore and stretch beyond their current capacity so they reach higher levels of the game. The work of Wilson and colleagues (2019) has now quantified this to be roughly 15 percent in order to maximize learning. Think of the implications in our classrooms if that struggle were embraced and not labeled as failure. This aligns with our previously mentioned view of rigor, an oft-debated concept in our profession, as that place just beyond where a student currently resides. Given this definition, rigor would therefore be available to every student from kindergarten through grade 12 and at every point of the learning continuum, from fully competent to not yet comprehending.

How, then, can we embrace this notion in our classrooms? The first step might be to consider how you view the schooling experience. As asked in chapter 2 (page 33), do you and your colleagues view school as a thirteen-year (K–12) experience or thirteen ten-month experiences? If it's the former, then we won't panic if a student doesn't achieve a certain learning target assigned to a grade level or content area because we know that, if it's essential (need to know), we will ensure they have learned it before they leave school. If it's the latter, we might be more inclined to panic as a ten-month segment draws to a close and the student has not mastered the learning target. While most educators (and likely most noneducators) would agree that literacy and numeracy are necessary skills to function in the adult world (we might also add mindsets, executive functioning skills, and broader behavioral skills), it's not likely that each grade level's content-area learning targets would carry the same weight. When looking at the totality of the school experience and not ten-month segments, it becomes easier to focus on the attributes and the time we have for all students to thoroughly learn the essentials. Struggle should be an accepted part of learning and not be seen as a synonym for failure.

This also connects to the notion that students should have multiple opportunities to show what they know. Let's move away from a one-shot attempt to demonstrate understanding, particularly if we have identified essential learning targets. Readers familiar with assessment work will recognize the idea of second chances or reassessment. We must allow our students to give their best effort, learn from that effort, commit to learning more, and then demonstrate their growth without fear of the failure label. The world is full of second-chance opportunities, and schools must stop being seen as the last bastion of the pass/fail dichotomy. It is entirely reasonable that we provide expectations around these second-chance opportunities by including the need to put in further effort and to demonstrate new knowledge before the next attempt is made. The renewed effort must be acknowledged if we hope to grow a student's ability and competence.

Realizing the Power of Lifelong Learning

Researcher Marjan Laal (2011) suggests that *lifelong learning* "comprises all phases of learning, from pre-school to post-retirement, and covers the whole spectrum of formal, non-formal and informal learning" (p. 470). Often, educators are advised to nurture lifelong learners. From the perspective of change over time, this makes sense. All educators are committed to continuous improvement for themselves and the profession. The knowledge gained on any topic since the 1970s would demand adjusting what and how we instruct and adding all we have learned about students and their capacity into our practice.

However, we need to move beyond this forced learning as a result of external change to embracing that we are all on a learning curve. This became very evident during the pandemic, when educators had to embrace an instant shift from delivering content live to delivering the same lessons in a virtual world. How much learning occurred for educators then? There were challenges that may have felt overwhelming, but the response was to overcome the challenge. This was a clear example of educators modeling lifelong learning and provides us lessons on the importance of lifelong learning that we ought to share with students. This also aligns with strengthening the mindset being discussed in this chapter.

A key to having a growth mindset is to believe in, and pursue, self-improvement. To be lifelong learners, individuals need to have a desire to develop their knowledge and skills beyond their formal education—to commit to continuing to grow at all stages in life. As mentioned previously, the current circumstances a student faces do not determine the end point; they just determine the starting point. Collectively, educators help students plot the course and inspire students to put forth the effort that will lead to the growth of their ability and competence. The support must be provided by educators to all students, wherever they are on the learning continuum, and with a variety of tools that come with the diverse skills available on school faculties.

Why Focus on "My Ability and Competence Grow With My Effort"?

This mindset seems like it should be readily embraced by all students and all educators. The notion of developing the desire to push for greater competency and ability would seemingly be aligned with the moral purpose of schools. Students with a growth mindset believe that "the brain is . . . like a muscle" that gets stronger with use (Dweck, 2016, p. 229). Moreover, students with a growth mindset are more likely to determine that academic challenges or mistakes are opportunities to learn and develop their brains. Having a growth mindset is also aligned to a desire to master the material, with students being motivated by their desire to learn as much as they can. As mentioned, students with a fixed mindset think of intelligence as something that is set and not something they have any control over (Dweck, 2016). Students with fixed mindsets are more likely to be performance oriented rather than mastery oriented. This view results in a desire to have the highest grade in comparison to their peers or to avoid any challenge that might make them look less intelligent by not measuring up to those same peers. Sadly, neither of these scenarios leads to the practice of the mindset being discussed in this chapter—the idea that effort and perseverance are essential to growing ability and competency. Students motivated to outperform others tend to give up quickly when success does not come easily, and those who are driven by the desire to hide what they fear is a substandard level of intelligence are likely to refrain from engaging in a task at all, lest they risk public failure, according to Lisa S. Blackwell, Kali H. Trzesniewski, and Carol S. Dweck (2007).

The previously mentioned research by Claro and colleagues (2016) also speaks to the very powerful notion that a belief in growth can even overcome the impacts of poverty on the learning process:

> Students from lower-income families were less likely to hold a growth mindset than their wealthier peers, but those who did hold a growth mindset were

> appreciably buffered against the deleterious effects of poverty on achievement: students in the lowest 10th percentile of family income who exhibited a growth mindset showed academic performance as high as that of fixed mindset students from the 80th income percentile. (p. 8664)

This is not to suggest that teaching students a growth mindset will alleviate the impacts of poverty and economic inequality. It does, however, speak to the power behind cultivating a mindset that does not add further challenges to those already brought on by the socioeconomic pressures faced.

One final piece of evidence to consider when determining the significance of this mindset comes once again from the work of Dweck (1986). In this early work, she speaks to the notion of working with students to have them attribute poor academic performance to a lack of effort or to the use of an ineffective strategy rather than a lack of ability. This "has been shown to produce sizable changes in persistence in the face of failure, changes that persist over time, and generalize across tasks" (Andrews & Debus, 1978, as cited in Colwell & Pollard, 2015, p. 39).

Fostering this mindset in our students and having them fully grasp that they can learn while also growing their competency and ability will not be easy. It will require some rethinking of how failure is viewed, how second opportunities are provided, and how educators and students work together to overcome some entrenched practices and viewpoints.

How Do We Nurture Students' Sense That "My Ability and Competence Grow With My Effort"?

The previous three chapters have detailed the important role teachers play in nurturing the first three positive mindsets. That role is equally important with this fourth mindset. This chapter makes the case that the intent is not to set up a dependency whereby we, the adults, must always be there for any success to occur. This mindset really speaks to developing the sense of independence and belief that effort is the key to growth. All learners are capable of effort, and all educators must be there to nurture and acknowledge that effort while connecting it deeply to the outcomes that are evident. In addition to giving students voice and choice (page 42), we can do so by teaching students about a growth mindset; embracing standards-based grading; praising students for effort instead of achievement alone; creating opportunities for students to take risks; helping students set achievable goals; and modeling confidence and resilience.

Teach Students About a Growth Mindset

The development of intrinsic motivation is often discussed in schools as a strong objective and a counter to students only being motivated by grades or other external rewards (Ryan & Deci, 2000). By educating our students about a growth mindset and how their effort can grow their ability and competence, educators may assist them in developing both a growth mindset and an increase in intrinsic motivation. In addition to explaining growth versus fixed mindsets to students, educators can use the following strategies to help teach about a growth mindset (Massachusetts Institute of Technology [MIT] Teaching and Learning Lab, n.d.).

- **Explain that everyone makes mistakes and fails at things:** There are individuals throughout history who achieved great success in life despite facing many failures and challenges along the way. The key is that they did not give up or let their failures define them. Instead, they used their failures as opportunities to learn, grow, and improve. Teachers could share some examples of famous failures who kept a growth mindset to overcome the temporary setbacks. For example, Thomas Edison (as cited in Dyer & Martin, 1910), who invented the light bulb, is attributed with this quote: "I have gotten a lot of results! I know several thousand things that won't work." Students may also be familiar with infamous NBA player Michael Jordan, who did not make the varsity high school basketball team (Hehir, 2020). This was a pivotal moment for him, as he could have easily given up at that point but instead became one of the dominant basketball players in the history of the sport.

- **Vocalize admiration when students show effort and use study strategies:** This may be as simple as the notion of catching someone at their best. Building resilience in your students may come from strategies such as the Three Before Me strategy (page 45). Recognizing and acknowledging effort goes a long way to boost a student's learning and prosocial behavior (Bennett, 2020). Providing a rubric of what is expected in an assignment can also guide them toward review and revision practices.

- **Normalize feedback being a critical part of learning:** Hattie and Helen Timperley (2007) define *feedback* as information provided to a learner relating to their skills or understanding as demonstrated on a task or in its completion, usually after instruction. Hattie and Timperley's model proposes that effective feedback must answer three key questions: "Where am I going?," "How am I going?," and "Where to next?" This takes practice for students to embrace that learning is an ongoing, iterative process and not just a final destination. Meta-analysis explains further that "feedback is more effective, the more information it contains" (Wisniewski, Zierer, & Hattie, 2019). Modeling this strategy happens when teachers are open to feedback from students about how they are learning and which strategies work and don't work.

Research scientist Betsy Ng (2018) explains the critical role teachers play in letting students know about the importance of and the value aligned with learning that "intelligence is malleable" by explaining that "teachers should also embrace a growth mindset [for themselves] such that they will understand the importance of providing autonomy over student learning to enhance self-regulation." In fact, research proves that:

> [Growth] mindset interventions may be ineffective if students are mostly operating in fixed-mindset environments. From the literature on mindset, we understand that student behaviors may be more tightly correlated with the instructor's mindset than students' own mindsets... Therefore, it is not enough for faculty and instructors to express a desire to have a growth mindset—their classroom practices and behaviors must also support the development of a growth mindset. (Park, Gunderson, Tsukayama, Levine, & Beilock, 2016 and Rattan, Good, & Dweck, 2012, as cited in MIT Teaching and Learning Lab, n.d.)

The development of this desire to learn, see the benefits of that learning, and push for more is the essence of lifelong learning and a recognition that learning is always available and not dependent on extrinsic rewards.

Use mindset surveys to know where student mindsets are. They need to know, too. The reproducible "Growth Mindset Survey for Students" (page 90) provides an opportunity for students to reflect and self-assess their mindsets, and "Student Growth Mindset Survey for Teachers' Assessment" (page 91) asks teachers to assess the mindsets of students in their class. The tools are mainly intended not to produce scores (although they do produce scores that can be tracked over time) but to provide a chance for reflection and the basis for discussion during student conferences. Use these surveys monthly.

Embrace Standards-Based Grading

Embracing standards-based mindsets—and assessment, grading, and feedback practices that increase hope, efficacy, achievement, and accuracy through standards-based grading—will enrich and inform a school's PLC and multitiered system of supports (MTSS) efforts and positively impact student mindsets. Educator and author Tom Schimmer's (2019) simple, clear definition for standards-based grading is *"grades based on the achievement of standards"* (emphasis in original). The practice breaks down large subjects into smaller learning objectives to help teachers better measure student learning. Sometimes this gets confused with proficiency-based or mastery-based grading, but those practices look more at a student's progress on a continuum of learning with mastery alluding to a higher level of achievement than proficiency.

When the following practices are in place, students will more powerfully see their role in their learning journey (thus enhancing their belief that "this work has value for me"), and their growth mindset will be enhanced because they see that the extra work they devote to learning concepts they have not yet learned pays off.

- Clear learning targets and success criteria
- Assessments that are aligned to learning targets
- Formative assessments that provide feedback to students and teachers prior to summative assessments
- Feedback that aligns to learning targets and is reported in proficiency levels (not percentages)
- Opportunities to continuously demonstrate growth in understanding
- Grades that authentically reflect what students know (not how they got there)

Schimmer's (2016) *Grading From the Inside Out: Bringing Accuracy to Student Assessment Through a Standards-Based Mindset* describes why and how to implement standards-based grading practices in schools and makes the connection between standards-based grading and mindsets.

Praise Students for Effort, Not Just Achievement

Teach students that it is OK to fail and that it is important to keep trying and continue to work hard. Let them know that you admire their persistence, reflection and relearning, thoughtful use of strategies in your classroom, or any other activity in which they are engaged. This helps them recognize their potential and build their confidence. Celebrating successes, big or small, also helps create a positive environment and encourages all students to keep trying and to keep striving for the best. By praising their efforts, you also remind them that diligence and dedication can bring success. Imagine this scenario: A student arrives to your grade and is assessed as three years behind in reading proficiency. If that student grows eighteen months under your tutelage, won't this be a wild success? The student is still behind the expected level, but their (and your) efforts have launched them into the world of possibility.

Create Opportunities for Students to Take Risks

By challenging students with activities that are slightly beyond their comfort zone, educators can help them learn to become more resilient and confident. This may mean encouraging them to try to master a new skill in physical education or a new game altogether. (Tom's daughter became a provincial champion in Netball, an unfamiliar sport until a teacher traveled to Australia.) It may mean learning a new language with a student from a different country serving as a mentor, or it may involve encouraging students to solve a problem in a different way. Whatever it is, create a safe and supportive environment in which students can take risks and learn to be brave.

Help Students Set Achievable Goals

Developing achievable goals helps students to focus on their strengths and set realistic milestones. It also helps to make progress measurable, and it encourages them to build on their success. When setting goals, make sure that the plans are realistic and achievable. You may even provide the necessary support and guidance to help the student reach the goal. And recognize that when students meet goals, their ability and competence are growing as a result of the efforts they have made to meet those goals. Reminding students of their progress toward goals is a way of nurturing a growth mindset.

Model Confidence and Resilience

Demonstrate your own ability to work through challenging situations. Doing so will model for students that no matter how hard things get, you can always find a way to persist. Remember the notion that if we don't model what we expect, we should expect what we do model. Most importantly, praise students' purposeful efforts and remind them that you believe in them and their capabilities. A practical way to do this is through the use of humor. Sharing a joke or having students share a joke is a good way to lighten the mood. In our work with schools, we occasionally get a chance to also work with students. Telling a few dad jokes always seems to get the sessions headed in the right direction. Find bright spots of the day through reflection and remind the class of things that sparked joy in all of them (Upp, 2023).

Action Items

Having reflected on the importance of students being able to positively say, "My ability and competence grow with my effort," consider which of the following action items you can tackle individually or with your colleagues to nurture this mindset broadly.

- Review the suggestions within the chapter in comparison to what your school and district are already doing so that you can possibly weave next steps into existing initiatives and commitments.
- Teach students about the way the brain learns and connect that learning to a growth mindset.
- Regularly begin lessons with the mindset minilessons, an example of which is in chapter 2 (figure 1.1, page 16), to make a growth mindset a central element of your learning environment.
- Use strategies to model that mistakes will occur, but that they are important and inevitable opportunities to learn and grow. The My Favorite Mistake strategy, for example, involves building in conversations that focus on and review a "favorite mistake," or an interesting error made by a student (or you) that caused some great learning and reflection.
- Learn about standards-based grading, embrace a standards-based mindset, and begin to introduce a few elements of standards-based grading to your school and classroom.
- Engage in professional learning—this book and its resource guides may help your efforts.

The reproducible "'My Ability and Competence Grow With My Effort' Action Plan" (page 94) helps teams hold collaborative conversations, guided by this action plan, to reflect on where they are and identify next steps they can take.

Growth Mindset Survey for Students

This survey measures a person's growth mindset (Dweck, 2016). For each statement, please choose one of the following ratings based on your current feelings.

1 = Always true   2 = Mostly true   3 = Sometimes true   4 = Never true

Belief	Rating
I feel connected to students at school.	
I feel connected to the adults at school.	
There are subject areas or other parts of school that are interesting and important to me.	
I see examples of people like me in my classroom and in my schoolwork.	
I can succeed in school.	
My teachers help me feel successful on assignments and in school.	
School is relevant to my life.	
I have chances to be involved in the parts of school that affect me.	
I get chances to be involved in my own learning.	
Adults at school ask for my opinions about my learning and about the school.	
It's possible to change how intelligent you are.	
I know if I put the time and effort in, I can get better at *anything* (sports, subject areas, and so on).	
When I make a mistake, I try to learn from it.	
I don't compare my grades and ability to those of my classmates.	
I enjoy getting out of my comfort zone.	
When I know I've put in my *best* effort, I feel successful regardless of what others think.	
I feel inspired by the success of others.	
I am inspired to keep going at something when I see my classmates being successful at that thing.	
Smart isn't something you are. Smart is something you become.	
I enjoy taking on a new challenge.	

Reference

Dweck, C. S. (2016). *Mindset: The new psychology of success* (Updated ed.). New York: Random House.

Source: © 2024 by Irvine Unified School District, Irvine, California. Used with permission.

Student Mindset Assessment for Teachers

The following survey has questions about each of the following four mindsets (from Farrington et al., 2012, p. 9).

1. "I belong in this academic community."
2. "I can succeed at this."
3. "This work has value for me."
4. "My ability and competence grow with my effort."

Teachers indicate, with a checkmark, which of the profiles matches a student for each mindset.

Indicators	Check for Yes
"I belong in this academic community."	
This student seems disconnected from school. This student is not engaged in class or activities; does not seem to be connected to any staff members or to other students; reports feeling like they do not belong; behaves in ways that indicate that they do not feel belonging.	
This student seems to like school but is not very involved. This student is sometimes engaged in class and activities; seems connected to a few adults on campus and to a few other students; sometimes reports feeling like they do not belong; behaves in ways that indicate they do not always feel belonging.	
This student is engaged in class. This student often participates in activities outside of class; connects to many adults on campus and a large group of peers; reports feeling like they belong; behaves in ways that indicate belonging.	
This student is highly participative in class and is a leader in the classroom and the school. This student is highly engaged in class and in many activities outside of class; seems connected to every adult on campus and nearly all other students; reports feeling belonging; behaves in ways that indicate that they feel belonging.	

Indicators	Check for Yes
"I can succeed at this."	
This student seems to lack confidence in their ability to learn. This student regularly shows no effort or perseverance; says, "I can't do this"; does not advocate for assistance; sits quietly without doing work or disrupts others in an effort to avoid work.	
This student is hesitant in their learning and when beginning a new assignment. This student may start an assignment but stop when encountering a challenge; says, "I don't get it"; asks others for help but is usually looking for an answer instead of further instruction; may turn in an assignment incomplete and move on to a preferred activity.	
This student generally believes in their abilities to learn and complete work successfully. This student, when faced with a difficult problem or tricky concept, sometimes expresses doubt and shows frustration, but gets back on track with redirection and assistance; sometimes seems surprised by their success.	
This student believes confidently, but not overconfidently, in their ability to learn. This student, when faced with a difficult problem or a tricky concept, refocuses and perseveres, even if it takes quite a bit of time; is sought out by other students for assistance.	
"This work has value for me."	
This student seems disengaged from school. This student shows the attitude that school doesn't matter and they don't like being there; does not want to be a part of class discussions; when asked their opinions, does not provide a constructive response; does not take advantage of choices or opportunities to be involved in learning.	
This student sometimes makes connections between school and the future but just as often views school as a chore. This student sometimes contributes to class discussions about the school, rules, and expectations but sometimes is disinterested; rarely takes advantage of choices or opportunities to take responsibility for learning.	
This student often makes connections between school and the future but sometimes seems to go through the motions. This student contributes to class discussions about the school, rules, and expectations but echoes others and follows the direction set by peers; generally takes advantage of choices and opportunities to take responsibility for learning.	
This student almost always volunteers connections between school and the future, seeming to embrace all parts of school with enthusiasm. This student leads class discussions about the school, rules, and expectations; encourages others, serving as an example for peers; embraces and takes full advantage of choices and opportunities to take responsibility for learning.	

Indicators	Check for Yes
"My ability and competence grow with my effort."	
This student strongly believes that their intelligence is fixed—it doesn't change much. If this student can't perform perfectly, they would rather not do something; thinks smart people don't have to work hard; does not display a belief in their abilities to grow as a student.	
This student leans toward thinking that their intelligence doesn't change much. This student prefers not to make mistakes if they can help it; doesn't really want to work too hard for it; may think that learning should be easy; occasionally displays a belief in their abilities to grow as a student.	
This student somewhat believes that their intelligence is something they can increase. This student cares about learning; is willing to work hard; wants to do well; thinks it's more important to learn than to always score well.	
This student really feels sure they can increase their intelligence by learning and likes a challenge. This student believes that the best way to learn is to work hard; doesn't mind making mistakes while they do it; consistently displays a belief in their abilities as a student.	

References

Dweck, C. S. (2016). *Mindset: The new psychology of success* (Updated ed.). New York: Random House.

Farrington, C. A., Roderick, M., Allensworth, E., Nagaoka, J., Keyes, T. S., Johnson, D. W., et al. (2012). *Teaching adolescents to become learners. The role of noncognitive factors in shaping school performance: A critical literature review.* Accessed at https://consortium.uchicago.edu/sites/default/files/2018-10/Noncognitive%20Report_0.pdf on November 13, 2023.

"My Ability and Competence Grow With My Effort" Action Plan

Among your collaborative teams, discuss these issues and create plans to address the ideas and suggestions recommended in this chapter.

Possible Action Area	Progress-Monitoring Suggestion	Next Steps
Teach Students About a Growth Mindset — In what ways can staff devote time to teaching the science and practice of a growth mindset and how it can lead to higher levels of achievement?	Examine assignments, resources, and assessments quarterly to evaluate whether they allow students to grow and learn from mistakes; determine if the connections in these items complement students engaging in and valuing the work and lead students to appreciate that effort matters and can produce satisfactory results.	
Ensure Voice, Choice, and Agency — How can staff demonstrate that school is not something done to students but instead is an experience in which they have agency?	Try some of this book's strategies to increase voice and choice (policy and practice involvement, classroom expectation creation, literature choice, physical education choice, and more) and monitor the impact they are having on your class culture.	

page 1 of 2

Positive Behaviors Start With Positive Mindsets © 2024 Solution Tree Press • SolutionTree.com
Visit **go.SolutionTree.com/behavior** to download this free reproducible.

Possible Action Area	Progress-Monitoring Suggestion	Next Steps
Embrace Standards-Based Grading What initial steps can teams employ to introduce elements of standards-based grading into their tasks, assessments, assignments, and grading so that student growth and progress over time is specifically, accurately, and fairly recorded?	Discuss what elements of standards-based grading might help your students achieve goals associated with learning, not just earning; survey students to determine their needs for more evidence related to growth rather than achievement alone.	
Encourage and Model a Growth Mindset In what ways can staff model their own growth mindset (Dweck, 2016) and communicate this mindset to students, and how can staff encourage and inspire students to adopt and embody a growth mindset?	Talk about your struggles and discuss ways to effectively communicate that with students so educators can model lifelong learning.	

Reference

Dweck, C. S. (2016). *Mindset: The new psychology of success* (Updated ed.). New York: Random House.

Epilogue

Our purpose in providing this resource is simple and straightforward. While this explanation appears throughout the book, it is repeated here: behavioral skills are as important as, or more important than, academic skills (Dweck et al., 2014). And mindsets are foundational to all other behavioral skills (Farrington et al., 2012). When schools make a commitment to nurturing student mindsets—to ensuring that all students feel like they belong, that they can succeed, that school and school experiences have a purpose and are relevant to their lives, and that their ability and competence will grow with effort—their social skills, perseverance, self-regulation, executive functioning, motivation, and academic performance will improve. The culture and climate of classrooms and the school will improve.

It starts with adult mindsets. In addition to teaching students about mindsets and creating environments, assignments, and experiences—such as those shared within the preceding four chapters—that nurture the four mindsets, adults must explicitly adopt and model these mindsets as well. After all, if you don't model what you expect, you should expect what you model. The work of educating students is the most important in the world. While it is challenging and can be exhausting, if the adults in schools do not feel as though they belong and do not fully commit to creating welcoming and inclusive classrooms and schools; if the adults do not fervently believe that all students can learn at high levels and do not craft the differentiated and scaffolded learning that ensure that this occurs; if the adults do not believe that schools are centers of communities and ought to be designed to be valuable and relevant places in which to grow; and if they do not embrace the notion that smart is not something that you are but something that all can become, then we can never hope, and should not expect, that students will display positive mindsets.

One of the wonderful aspects of the four mindsets is that they are actionable. As outlined in the four chapters of this book, explicit actions can make the shifts in schools and schoolwork to directly improve student mindsets.

Gathering information about and measuring improvements to student mindsets is important so that we can adjust our efforts and celebrate successes. Here are a few ways that we measure student mindsets.

- **Classroom environment surveys:** These surveys provide honest, powerful, and useful information to teachers on how students view the classroom environment, including the extent to which they see themselves in the class, feel comfortable in the class, and feel like they are part of the classroom community.

- **Attendance and tardies:** When measuring the impact of your efforts to increase the sense of belonging within the school community and the connections that students feel to peers, teachers, classes, content areas, and the school, don't neglect data that you already gather. When students feel more a part of the school and school community, they will arrive to school and classes on time more often and will attend school more consistently (Kumar et al., 2018).

- **Mindset surveys:** Included as an example at the end of chapter 4, the reproducible "Growth Mindset Survey for Students" (page 90) and "Student Growth Mindset Survey for Teachers' Assessment" (page 91) can reveal how students see their own mindset and how teachers see students' evolving mindsets.

- **Behavioral incidents:** When student mindsets improve, students' social behaviors will also improve. We should expect improvements in respect, responsibility, and kindness as students feel better about themselves and the school community.

- **Participation in extracurriculars:** After encouraging students to participate in clubs or activities outside of class, measure rates of participation and strive for improvements.

- **Analyses of journaling activities:** Review student responses to "Gratitude Journal Prompts" (page 27) to learn about students and their needs and to assess improvements in student attitudes and mindsets.

We fervently hope that you commit to the work of implementing practices and processes that nurture more positive and productive student mindsets. It is work that we can and must do. We hope that this resource provides the ideas and tools that you need to be successful in this endeavor.

References and Resources

Aldous, C. R. (2014). Attending to feeling: It may matter more than you think. *Creative Education*, *5*(10), 780–790.

Allen, K., Kern, M. L., Vella-Brodrick, D., Hattie, J., & Waters, L. (2018). What schools need to know about fostering school belonging: A meta-analysis. *Educational Psychology Review*, *30*(1), 1–34.

Allensworth, E. A., Farrington, C. A., Gordon, M. F., Johnson, D. W., Klein, K., McDaniel, B., et al. (2018). *Supporting social, emotional, and academic development: Research implications for educators*. Accessed at https://consortium.uchicago.edu/sites/default/files/2019-01/Supporting%20Social%20Emotional-Oct2018-Consortium.pdf on January 12, 2024.

Alter, P., & Haydon, T. (2017). Characteristics of effective classroom rules: A review of the literature. *Teacher Education and Special Education*, *40*(2), 114–127.

Andrews, G. R., & Debus, R. L. (1978). Persistence and the causal perception of failure: Modifying cognitive attributions. *Journal of Educational Psychology*, *70*(2), 154–166.

Ayers, S. (2014, February 17). *Under the surface* [Video file]. Accessed at www.youtube.com/watch?v=AZ-pU7ozt3g on March 24, 2024.

Bandura, A. (1977). Self-efficacy: Toward a unifying theory of behavioral change. *Psychological Review*, *84*(2), 191–215.

Bandura, A. (1986). *Social foundations of thought and action: A social cognitive theory*. Englewood Cliffs, NJ: Prentice Hall.

Barron, C. (2022, July 19). A perspective that promotes resilience [Blog post]. *Psychology Today*. Accessed at www.psychologytoday.com/us/blog/the-creativity-cure/202207/perspective-promotes-resilience on March 22, 2024.

Bennett, C. (2020). *Effective praise in the classroom*. Accessed at www.thoughtco.com/effective-praise-8161 on March 22, 2024.

Bennett, C. A. (2014). Creating cultures of participation to promote mathematical discourse. *Middle School Journal, 46*(2), 20–25.

Bjorklund, P., Jr. (2019). "Whoa. You speak Mexican?": Latina/o high school students' sense of belonging in Advanced Placement and honors classes. *Journal of Education for Students Placed at Risk (JESPAR), 24*(2), 109–131.

Blackwell, L. S., Trzesniewski, K. H., & Dweck, C. S. (2007). Implicit theories of intelligence predict achievement across an adolescent transition: A longitudinal study and an intervention. *Child Development, 78*(1), 246–263.

Blad, E. (2022). *Educators see gaps in kids' emotional growth due to pandemic.* Accessed at www.edweek.org/leadership/educators-see-gaps-in-kids-emotional-growth-due-to-pandemic/2022/02 on February 20, 2024.

Blake, C. (2015). *Teaching social justice in theory and practice.* Accessed at https://resilienteducator.com/classroom-resources/teaching-social-justice on March 24, 2024.

Borghans, L., Golsteyn, B. H. H., Heckman, J. J., & Humphries, J. E. (2016). What grades and achievement tests measure. *Proceedings of the National Academy of Sciences, 113*(47), 13354–13359. Accessed at https://doi.org/10.1073/pnas.1601135113 on March 30, 2024.

Bottiani, J. H., Bradshaw, C. P., & Mendelson, T. (2017). A multilevel examination of racial disparities in high school discipline: Black and white adolescents' perceived equity, school belonging, and adjustment problems. *Journal of Educational Psychology, 109*(4), 532–545.

Brady, L. M., Fryberg, S. A., & Shoda, Y. (2018). Expanding the interpretive power of psychological science by attending to culture. *Proceedings of the National Academy of Sciences, 115*(45), 11406–11413.

Branje, S., & Morris, A. S. (2021). The impact of the COVID-19 pandemic on adolescent emotional, social, and academic adjustment. *Journal of Adolescent Research, 31*(3), 486–499.

Bronk, K. C. (2012). A grounded theory of youth purpose. *Journal of Adolescent Research, 27,* 78–109.

Brooks, R. (2003). *Self-worth, resilience, and hope: The search for islands of competence.* Metairie, LA: The Center for Development and Learning.

Brophy, J. (2008). Developing students' appreciation for what is taught in school. *Educational Psychologist, 43,* 132–141.

Brown, J., & Wong, J. (2017). *How gratitude changes you and your brain.* Accessed at https://greatergood.berkeley.edu/article/item/how_gratitude_changes_you_and_your_brain on February 21, 2024.

Burrow, A. L., & Hill, P. L. (2011). Purpose as a form of identity capital for positive youth adjustment. *Developmental Psychology, 47,* 1196–1206.

Calderon, V. J., & Yu, D. (2017). *Student enthusiasm falls as high school graduation nears.* Accessed at https://news.gallup.com/opinion/gallup/211631/student-enthusiasm-falls-high-school-graduation-nears.aspx on November 13, 2023.

California Department of Education. (2023). *Mathematics framework for California public schools: Kindergarten through grade twelve.* Accessed at www.cde.ca.gov/ci/ma/cf/ on January 4, 2024.

California Safe and Supportive Schools & WestEd. (2020). *Teacher support: High expectations and caring relationships.* Accessed at https://ca-safe-supportive-schools.wested.org/wp-content/uploads/2020/10/S3factsheet1_caring_20120223.pdf on January 12, 2024.

Chew, S. L. (2022). *Cognitive goals for class: Academic mindset.* Accessed at www.teachingprofessor.com/free-article/cognitive-goals-for-class-academic-mindset on March 21, 2024.

Chiu, M. M., Chow, B. W.-Y., McBride, C., & Mol, S. T. (2016). Students' sense of belonging at school in 41 countries: Cross-cultural variability. *Journal of Cross-Cultural Psychology, 47*(2), 175–196.

Claro, S., Paunesku, D., & Dweck, C. S. (2016). Growth mindset tempers the effects of poverty on academic achievement. *Proceedings of the National Academy of Sciences, 113*(31), 8664–8668. Accessed at https://doi.org/10.1073/pnas.1608207113 on March 30, 2024.

Cobb, F., & Krownapple, J. (2019). *Belonging through a culture of dignity: The keys to successful equity implementation.* San Diego, CA: Mimi & Todd Press.

Cohen, G. L., & Garcia, J. (2014). Educational theory, practice, and policy and the wisdom of social psychology. *Policy Insights From the Behavioral and Brain Sciences, 1*(1), 13–20.

Cohen, G. L., & Sherman, D. (2014). The psychology of change: Self-affirmation and social psychological intervention. *Annual Review of Psychology, 65*, 333–371.

Cohen, G. L., & Steele, C. M. (2002). A barrier of mistrust: How negative stereotypes affect cross-race mentoring. In J. Aronson (Ed.), *Improving academic achievement: Impact of psychological factors on education* (pp. 303–327). Cambridge, MA: Academic Press. Accessed at https://doi.org/10.1016/B978-012064455-1/50018-X on March 30, 2024.

Collaborative for Academic, Social, and Emotional Learning. (n.d.). *What is the CASEL framework?* Accessed at https://casel.org/fundamentals-of-sel/what-is-the-casel-framework on April 5, 2024.

Colwell, J., & Pollard, A. (Eds.) (2015). *Readings for reflective teaching in early education* (2nd ed.). London: Bloomsbury Academic.

Conner, J., Posner, M., & Nsowaa, B. (2022). The relationship between student voice and student engagement in urban high schools. *Urban Review, 54*, 755–774. Accessed at https://doi.org/10.1007/s11256-022-00637-2 on March 30, 2024.

Covarrubias, R., & Fryberg, S. A. (2015). The impact of self-relevant representations on school belonging for Native American students. *Cultural Diversity and Ethnic Minority Psychology, 21*(1), 10–18.

Croce, K. M., & Salter, J. S. (2022). Beyond the walls: Establishing classroom expectations in a virtual classroom. *Frontiers in Education, 7*, 1–6.

Dalakas, V. (2016). Turning guest speakers' visits into active learning opportunities. *Atlantic Marketing Journal, 5*(2), 93–100.

Daniels, H. (2017). *The curious classroom.* Portsmouth, NH: Heinemann.

Del Castillo, N. (2022). *How gratitude promotes inclusivity.* Accessed at https://mentalhealth.uiowa.edu/news/2022/11/how-gratitude-promotes-inclusivity on February 22, 2024.

Doménech-Betoret, F., Abellán-Roselló, L., & Gómez-Artiga, A. (2017). Self-efficacy, satisfaction, and academic achievement: The mediator role of students' expectancy-value beliefs. *Frontiers in Psychology, 8,* 1193.

Duckworth, A. L., & Carlson, S. M. (2013). Self-regulation and school success. In B. W. Sokol, F. M. E. Grouzet, & U. Müller (Eds.), *Self-regulation and autonomy: Social and developmental dimensions of human conduct* (pp. 208–230). New York: Cambridge University Press.

Duckworth, A. L., Quinn, P. D., & Tsukayama, E. (2012). What No Child Left Behind leaves behind: The roles of IQ and self-control in predicting standardized achievement test scores and report card grades. *Journal of Educational Psychology, 104*(2), 439–451. Accessed at https://doi.org/10.1037/a0026280 on March 30, 2024.

Duckworth, A. L., & Seligman, M. E. P. (2005). Self-discipline outdoes IQ in predicting academic performance of adolescents. *Psychological Science, 16*(12), 939–944. Accessed at https://doi.org/10.1111/j.1467-9280.2005.01641.x on March 30, 2024.

Dweck, C. (2015, September 22). *Carol Dweck revisits the "growth mindset."* Accessed at www.edweek.org/leadership/opinion-carol-dweck-revisits-the-growth-mindset/2015/09 on March 24, 2024.

Dweck, C. S. (1986). Motivational processes affecting learning. *American Psychologist, 41,* 1046.

Dweck, C. S. (2013). *Self-theories: Their role in motivation, personality, and development.* London: Psychology Press.

Dweck, C. S. (2014). *Self-theories: Their role in motivation, personality, and development* (2nd ed.). New York: Taylor & Francis.

Dweck, C. S. (2016). *Mindset: The new psychology of success* (Updated ed.). New York: Random House.

Dweck, C. S., Walton, G. M., & Cohen, G. L. (2014). *Academic tenacity: Mindsets and skills that promote long-term learning.* Seattle, WA: Bill & Melinda Gates Foundation.

Dweck, C. S., & Yeager, D. S. (2019). Mindsets: A view from two eras. *Perspectives on Psychological Science: A Journal of the Association for Psychological Science, 14*(3), 481–496.

Dyer, F. L., & Martin, T. C. (1910). *Edison, his life and inventions.* Accessed at www.gutenberg.org/files/820/820-h/820-h.htm on March 22, 2024.

Farrington, C. A., Roderick, M., Allensworth, E., Nagaoka, J., Keyes, T. S., Johnson, D. W., et al. (2012). *Teaching adolescents to become learners. The role of noncognitive factors in shaping school performance: A critical literature review.* Accessed at https://consortium.uchicago.edu/sites/default/files/2018-10/Noncognitive%20Report_0.pdf on November 13, 2023.

Fuligni, A. J. (2019). The need to contribute during adolescence. *Perspectives on Psychological Science, 14*(3), 331–343.

Garcia, J., & Cohen, G. L. (2012). A social-psychological approach to educational intervention. In E. Shafir (Ed.), *Behavioral foundations of policy* (pp. 329–350). Princeton, NJ: Princeton University Press.

Geers, A. L., Weiland, P. E., Kosbab, K., Landry, S. J., & Helfer, S. G. (2005). Goal activation, expectations, and the placebo effect. *Journal of Personality and Social Psychology, 89*(2), 143.

Goddard, R., Hoy, W., & Hoy, A. W. (2004). Collective efficacy beliefs: Theoretical developments, empirical evidence, and future directions. *Educational Researcher, 33*(3), 3–13.

Goodman, J. F., & Eren, N. S. (2013). Student agency: Success, failure, and lessons learned. *Ethics and Education, 8*(2), 123–139.

Gopalan, M., & Brady, S. T. (2020). College students' sense of belonging: A national perspective. *Educational Researcher, 49*(2), 134–137.

Graham, M., Wayne, I., Persutte-Manning, S., Pergantis, S., & Vaughan, A. (2022). Enhancing student outcomes: Peer mentors and student transition. *International Journal of Teaching and Learning in Higher Education, 34*(1), 1812–9129.

Gray, D. L. (2017). Is psychological membership in the classroom a function of standing out while fitting in? Implications for achievement motivation and emotions. *Journal of School Psychology, 61*, 103–121.

Gray, D. L., McElveen, T. L., Green, B. P., & Bryant, L. H. (2020). Engaging Black and Latinx students through communal learning opportunities: A relevance intervention for middle schoolers in STEM elective classrooms. *Contemporary Educational Psychology, 60*, 101833. Accessed at https://doi.org/10.1016/j.cedpsych.2019.101833 on March 30, 2024.

Greenfield, J. (2022). Toward a purpose-first model of postsecondary support. *Phi Delta Kappan, 103*(8), 37–42.

Harackiewicz, J. M., Rozek, C. R., Hulleman, C. S., & Hydes, J. S. (2012). Helping parents to motivate adolescents in mathematics and science: An experimental test of a utility-value intervention. *Psychological Science, 23*, 899–906.

Harackiewicz, J. M., Smith, J. L., & Priniski, S. J. (2016). Interest matters: The importance of promoting interest in education. *Policy Insights From the Behavioral and Brain Sciences, 3*(2), 200–227.

Hattie, J. (2012). *Visible learning for teachers: Maximizing impact on learning.* Abingdon, England: Routledge.

Hattie, J. (2023). *Visible learning, the sequel: A synthesis of over 2,100 meta-analyses relating to achievement.* Abingdon, England: Routledge.

Hattie, J., & Gan, M. (2011). *Handbook of research on learning and instruction.* Abingdon, England: Routledge.

Hattie, J., Gan, M., & Brooks, C. (2016). Instruction based on feedback. In R. E. Mayer & P. A. Alexander (Eds.), *Handbook of research on learning and instruction* (2nd ed., pp. 290–324). Oxfordshire, England: Routledge.

Hattie, J., & Timperley, H. (2007). The power of feedback. *Review of Educational Research, 77*(1), 81–112. Accessed at https://doi.org/10.3102/003465430298487 on March 30, 2024.

Heckman, J. J., & Kautz, T. (2012). Hard evidence on soft skills. *Labour Economics, 19*(4), 451–464. Accessed at https://doi.org/10.1016/j.labeco.2012.05.014 on March 30, 2024.

Hehir, J. (Director). (2020). *The last dance* [Film]. Netflix.

Hierck, T. (2017). *Seven keys to a positive learning environment in your classroom.* Bloomington, IN: Solution Tree Press.

Hierck, T., & Freese, A. (2018). *Assessing unstoppable learning.* Bloomington, IN: Solution Tree Press.

Hill, P. L., Burrow, A. L., & Sumner, R. (2013). Addressing important questions in the field of adolescent purpose. *Child Development Perspectives, 7*, 232–236.

Im, M. H., Hughes, J. N., Cao, Q., & Kwok, O. (2016). Effects of extracurricular participation during middle school on academic motivation and achievement at grade 9. *American Educational Research Journal, 53*(5), 1343–1375.

Immordino-Yang, M. H., & Faeth, M. (2010). The role of emotion and skilled intuition in learning. In D. A. Sousa (Ed.), *Mind, brain, and education* (2nd ed, pp. 69–84). Bloomington, IN: Solution Tree Press.

Johnson, S. (1750). The rambler, *15*(1). In S. Johnson (Ed.), *Moore's British classics: Containing Dr. Johnson's rambler, and Lord Littleton's Persian letters* (Vol. 1, No. 25). Farmington Hills, MI: Gale ECCO.

Jones, S. M., & Doolittle, E. J. (2017). Social and emotional learning: Introducing the issue. *The Future of Children, 27*(1), 3–11.

Kim, J. (2021). The quality of social relationships in schools and adult health: Differential effects of student–student versus student–teacher relationships. *School Psychology, 36*(1), 6–16.

King, A. E., McQuarrie, F. A. E., & Brigham, S. M. (2021). Exploring the relationship between student success and participation in extracurricular activities. *SCHOLE: A Journal of Leisure Studies and Recreation Education, 36*(1–2), 42–58.

Kolb, A. Y., & Kolb, D. A. (2009). Experiential learning theory: A dynamic, holistic approach to management learning, education and development. In S. J. Armstrong & C. V. Fukami (Eds.), *The SAGE handbook of management learning, education and development* (pp. 42–68). Thousand Oaks, CA: SAGE.

Kuhfeld, M., Soland, J., Lewis, K., & Morton, E. (2022). *The pandemic has had devastating impacts on learning. What will it take to help students catch up?* Accessed at https://ies.ed.gov/ncee/edlabs/regions/west/pdf/REL_2017226.pdf on February 24, 2024.

Kumar, R., Zusho, A., & Bondie, R. (2018). Weaving cultural relevance and achievement motivation into inclusive classroom cultures. *Educational Psychologist, 53*(2), 78–96.

Laal, M. (2011). Lifelong learning: What does it mean? *Procedia—Social and Behavioral Sciences, 28*, 470–474. Accessed at https://doi.org/10.1016/j.sbspro.2011.11.090 on March 30, 2024.

Limeri, L. B., Carter, N. T., Choe, J., Harper, H. G., Martin, H. R., Benton, A., et al. (2020). Growing a growth mindset: Characterizing how and why undergraduate students' mindsets change. *International Journal of STEM Education, 7*, 35. Accessed at https://doi.org/10.1186/s40594-020-00227-2 on March 30, 2024.

Maloney, T., & Matthews, J. S. (2020). Teacher care and students' sense of connectedness in the urban mathematics classroom. *Journal for Research in Mathematics Education, 51*(4), 399–432.

Martin, A. J., Burns, E. C., Collie, R. J., Bostwick, K. C. P., Flesken, A., & McCarthy, I. (2022). Growth goal setting in high school: A large-scale study of perceived instructional support, personal background attributes, and engagement outcomes. *Journal of Educational Psychology, 14*(4), 752–771.

Marzano, R. J. (2017). *The new art and science of teaching* (Rev. and expanded ed.). Bloomington, IN: Solution Tree Press.

Maslow, A. H. (2013). *A theory of human motivation.* Eastford, CT: Martino Fine Books. (Original work published 1943)

Massachusetts Institute of Technology Teaching and Learning Lab. (n.d.). *Growth mindset.* Accessed at https://tll.mit.edu/teaching-resources/inclusive-classroom/growth-mindset on February 21, 2024.

Minahan, J. (2019). Trauma-informed teaching strategies. *Educational Leadership, 77*(2), 30–35. Accessed at https://eric.ed.gov/?id=EJ1231183 on March 30, 2024.

Mitra, D. (2018). Student voice in secondary schools: The possibility for deeper change. *Journal of Educational Administration, 56*(5), 473–487.

Morales-Chicas, J., & Graham, S. (2017). Latinos' changing ethnic group representation from elementary to middle school: Perceived belonging and academic achievement. *Journal of Research on Adolescence, 27*(3), 537–549.

Murphy, M. C., Gopalan, M., Carter, E. R., Emerson, K. T. U., Bottoms, B. L., & Walton, G. M. (2020). A customized belonging intervention improves retention of socially disadvantaged students at a broad-access university. *Science Advances, 6*(29). Accessed at www.science.org/doi/10.1126/sciadv.aba4677 on March 30, 2024.

National Governors Association Center for Best Practices & Council of Chief State School Officers. (2010). *Common Core State Standards for mathematics*. Washington, DC: Authors. Accessed at https://learning.ccsso.org/wp-content/uploads/2022/11/ADA-Compliant-Math-Standards.pdf on April 5, 2024.

Ng, B. (2018). The neuroscience of growth mindset and intrinsic motivation. *Brain Sciences, 8*(2), 20.

Noftle, E. E., & Robins, R. W. (2007). Personality predictors of academic outcomes: Big five correlates of GPA and SAT scores. *Journal of Personality and Social Psychology, 93*(1), 116–130. Accessed at https://doi.org/10.1037/0022-3514.93.1.116 on March 30, 2024.

O'Brien, K. A., & Bowles, T. V. (2013). The importance of belonging for adolescents in secondary school settings. *The European Journal of Social and Behavioural Sciences, 5*(2), 976–984.

Organisation for Economic Co-operation and Development. (n.d.). *Student agency for 2030*. Accessed at www.oecd.org/education/2030-project/teaching-and-learning/learning/student-agency/Student_Agency_for_2030_concept_note.pdf on February 21, 2024.

Osher, D., & Kendziora, K. (2010). *Building conditions for learning and healthy adolescent development: A strategic approach. Handbook of youth prevention science*. Accessed at www.researchgate.net/publication/292710707_Building_conditions_for_learning_and_healthy_adolescent_development_A_strategic_approach on November 13, 2023.

Oyserman, D., & James, L. (2009). Possible selves: From content to process. In K. D. Markman, W. M. P. Klein, & J. A. Suhr (Eds.), *The handbook of imagination and mental simulation* (pp. 373–394). New York: Psychology Press.

Park, D., Gunderson, E. A., Tsukayama, E., Levine, S. C., & Beilock, S. L. (2016). Young children's motivational frameworks and math achievement: Relation to teacher-reported instructional practices, but not teacher theory of intelligence. *Journal of Educational Psychology, 108*(3), 300–313. Accessed at http://doi.org/10.1037/edu0000064 on March 30, 2024.

Pearson, J. A. (2023). *Empowering students for success: 12 practical strategies to promote student agency*. Accessed at www.amisa.us/post/12-practical-strategies-to-promote-student-agency on February 21, 2024.

Poropat, A. E. (2009). A meta-analysis of the five-factor model of personality and academic performance. *Psychological Bulletin, 135*(2), 322–338. Accessed at https://doi.org/10.1037/a0014996 on March 30, 2024.

Putwain, D., Sander, P., & Larkin, D. (2013). Academic self-efficacy in study-related skills and behaviours: Relations with learning-related emotions and academic success. *British Journal of Educational Psychology, 83*(4), 633–650.

Rattan, A., Good, C., & Dweck, C. S. (2012). "It's ok—Not everyone can be good at math": Instructors with an entity theory comfort (and demotivate) students. *Journal of Experimental Social Psychology*, *48*(3), 731–737. Accessed at http://doi.org/10.1016/j.jesp.2011.12.012 on March 30, 2024.

Robinson, C. (2018). Guest speakers and mentors for career exploration in the science classroom. *Science Scope*, *4*(8), 18–21.

Rodriguez-Monge, M., Isabela, I., & Chiappelli, F. (2023). COVID-19 effects on social-emotional development: Impact of early intervention. *Bioinformation*, *19*(9), 889–892.

Rubie-Davies, C. M., Peterson, E. R., Sibley, C. G., & Rosenthal, R. (2015). A teacher expectation intervention: Modelling the practices of high expectation teachers. *Contemporary Educational Psychology*, *40*, 72–85.

Ryan, R. M., & Deci, E. L. (2000). Intrinsic and extrinsic motivations: Classic definition and new directions. *Contemporary Educational Psychology*, *25*(1), 54–67.

Sadi, O., & Uyar, M. (2013). The relationship between self-efficacy, self-regulated learning strategies and achievement: A path model. *Journal of Baltic Science Education*, *12*(1), 21–33.

Schimmer, T. (2016). *Grading from the inside out: Bringing accuracy to student assessment through a standards-based mindset*. Bloomington, IN: Solution Tree Press.

Schimmer, T. (2019, March 11). Standards-based grading: A million little things [Blog post]. *All Things Assessment*. Accessed at https://allthingsassessment.info/2019/03/11/standards-based-grading-a-million-little-things on March 22, 2024.

Schlechty, P. C. (1997). *Inventing better schools: An action plan for educational reform*. San Francisco: Jossey-Bass.

Seita, J. (2014). Reclaiming disconnected kids. *Reclaiming Children and Youth*, *23*(1), 28–32.

Shiff, L., & Johnson, B. (2021). *What I'm feeling is okay!* St. Paul, MN: Beaver's Pond Press.

Sileo, F. J., & Zivoin, J. (2017). *A world of plausibilities: An exercise in mindfulness*. Washington, DC: Magination.

Snipes, J., & Jacobson, A. (2021). *Academic mindsets and behaviors, prior achievement, and the transition to middle school* (REL 2022–123). Washington, DC: U.S. Department of Education, Institute of Education Sciences, National Center for Education Evaluation and Regional Assistance, Regional Educational Laboratory West. Accessed at https://files.eric.ed.gov/fulltext/ED615451.pdf on December 13, 2023.

Snipes, J., & Tran, L. (2017). *Growth mindset, performance avoidance, and academic behaviors in Clark County School District* (REL 2017–226). Washington, DC: U.S. Department of Education, Institute of Education Sciences, National Center for Education Evaluation and Regional Assistance, Regional Educational Laboratory West. Accessed at https://ies.ed.gov/ncee/edlabs/regions/west/pdf/REL_2017226.pdf on December 13, 2023.

Southern Poverty Law Center. (2018). *Social justice standards: The Teaching Tolerance anti-bias framework*. Accessed at www.learningforjustice.org/sites/default/files/2020-09/TT-Social-Justice-Standards-Anti-bias-framework-2020.pdf on Mach 24, 2024.

Steger, M. F. (2012). Experiencing meaning in life: Optimal functioning at the nexus of spirituality, psychopathology, and well-being. In P. T. P. Wong (Ed.), *The human quest for meaning* (2nd ed., pp. 165–184). New York: Routledge.

Steger, M. F., Bundick, M., & Yeager, D. S. (2012). The development of meaning during adolescence. In R. J. Levesque (Ed.), *Encyclopedia of adolescence* (pp. 1666–1777). New York: Springer Press.

Storyhive. (2017). *Yoga for kids!* [Video file]. Accessed at https://www.youtube.com/watch?v=X655B4ISakg on February 20, 2024.

Subramaniam, S., & Prabhat, S. (2022). *Namaste is a greeting*. Somerville, MA: Candlewick.

Upp, A. (2023). *3 ways I model resilience for my students*. Accessed at www.understood.org/en/articles/3-ways-i-model-resilience-for-my-students on March 24, 2024.

Vaughn, M. (2018). Making sense of student agency in the early grades. *Phi Delta Kappan, 99*(7), 62–66.

Vaughn, M. (2020). What is student agency and why is it needed now more than ever? *Theory Into Practice, 59*(2), 109–118.

Villavicencio, F. T., & Bernardo, A. B. (2013) Negative emotions moderate the relationship between self-efficacy and achievement of Filipino students. *Psychological Studies, 58*(3), 225–232.

Virgil. (70–19 BC). *Aeneid: Book V*. Accessed at www.perseus.tufts.edu/hopper/text-?doc=Perseus%3Atext%3A1999.02.0054%3Abook%3D5 on April 9, 2024.

Vygotsky, L. S. (1978). *Mind in society: The development of higher psychological processes*. Cambridge, MA: Harvard University Press.

Vygotsky, L. S. (1997). *The collected works of L. S. Vygotsky: Vol. 3. Problems of the theory and history of psychology* (R. W. Rieber & J. Wollock, Eds.). New York: Plenum Press.

Walton, G. M., & Brady, S. T. (2017). The many questions of belonging. In *Handbook of competence and motivation: Theory and application* (2nd ed., pp. 272–293). New York: Guilford Press.

Walton, G. M., & Cohen, G. L. (2007). A question of belonging: Race, social fit, and achievement. *Journal of Personality and Social Psychology, 92*(1), 82–96.

Walton, G. M., & Cohen, G. L. (2011). A brief social-belonging intervention improves academic and health outcomes of minority students. *Science, 331*(6023), 1447–1451.

Wilson, R. C., Shenhav, A., Straccia, M., & Cohen, J. D. (2019). The eighty five percent rule for optimal learning. *Nature Communications, 10*, 4646. Accessed at https://doi.org/10.1038/s41467-019-12552-4 on March 30, 2024.

Wisniewski, B., Zierer, K., & Hattie, J. (2019). The power of feedback revisited: A meta-analysis of educational feedback research. *Frontiers in Psychology, 10*, 3087. Accessed at www.frontiersin.org/journals/psychology/articles/10.3389/fpsyg.2019.03087/full on March 22, 2024.

Woodson, J., & López, R. (2022). *The year we learned to fly*. New York: Nancy Paulsen Books.

Yeager, D. S., Bundick, M. J., & Johnson, R. (2012). The role of future work goal motives in adolescent identity development: A longitudinal mixed-methods investigation. *Contemporary Educational Psychology, 37,* 206–217.

Yu, M. V. B., Johnson, H. E., Deutsch, N. L., & Varga, S. M. (2018). "She calls me by my last name": Exploring adolescent perceptions of positive teacher-student relationships. *Journal of Adolescent Research, 33*(3), 332–362.

Index

A
academic behaviors, 2, 3
achievement
    feedback and, 43
    growth versus achievement, 36–37
    praising effort, 87–88
    sense of belonging and, 11
    standards-based grading and, 87
    status, definition of, 36
Ainsworth, L., 43
agency, 60, 62, 69
assessments
    customizing, 72
    giving specific feedback and, 43–44
    standards-based grading and, 87
attendance, 98

B
balanced breathing, 49
balloon belly breathing, 49
Bandura, A., 33
behavior
    academic behaviors, 2, 3
    behavioral incidents, 98
    categories of, 2–3
    importance of behavioral skills, 97
belonging. *See also "I belong in this academic community" mindset*
    as a focus, 10–12
    meaning of, 10
    nurturing a sense of, 12–18

box breathing, 49
breaking it up, 50

C
California Department of Education, 62
categories of behavior, 2–3
check-in/check-out (CICO), 17–18, 29
choice and voice, 42–43
chunking, 50
Claro, S., 39, 83–84
classroom commitments, 65
classroom environment survey, 98
classroom meetings, 13–14, 15
clubs and activities
    encouraging extracurriculars, 72–73
    nurturing a sense of belonging and, 18
community and comfort, 13–14
compacts, 63–66
confidence, modeling, 88–89
connectedness. *See "I belong in this academic community" mindset*
curriculum, customizing, 72

D
differentiated instruction, 44
Dweck, C. S., 39, 60

E
Edison, T., 85
effort, praising, 85, 87–88
environmental surveys, 17, 98
executive functioning, use of term, 1

expectations
    allowing voice and choice, 42–43
    classroom expectations, 42, 64–65
    feedback and, 43–44
    growth mindset and, 44
    impact of, 40–41
    letting them know (and believing it yourself), 42
    making expectations clear, realistic, and reasonable, 44–45
extracurriculars, 72–73, 98

F

failure
    framing mistakes and struggles, 45–46
    growth mindset and, 85
    reframing failure, 49–50
    understanding as key to rigor, 80–82
Farrington, C., 2, 38
feedback
    expectations and, 43–44, 65
    feedback loops, 47
    growth mindset and, 85–86
fixed mindset, 79, 83
Freese, A., 36, 37

G

goals
    agency and, 62
    assessment data and, 43–44
    connecting to a purpose for learning, 67–69
    "I can succeed at this" mindset and, 47, 49
    setting achievable goals, 88
    short- and long-term goals for elementary and secondary students, 68
gratitude journals
    measuring progress and success, 49
    nurturing a sense of belonging and, 17
    reproducibles for, 27–28
growth mindset. *See also "My ability and competence grow with my effort" mindset*
    expectations and, 44
    poverty and, 39, 83–84
    teaching students about, 85–86
growth versus achievement, 36–37
guest speakers, 64

H

Hattie, J., 41
Hierck, T., 36, 37
high expectations, 40–45. *See also expectations*

I

"I belong in this academic community" mindset
    about, 9
    action items, 19
    focusing on, 10–12
    learning targets, 8
    meaning of, 10
    nurturing, 12–18
    reproducibles for, 20–31
"I can succeed at this" mindset. *See also self-efficacy*
    about, 33–34
    action items, 50–51
    focusing on, 38–40
    learning targets, 32
    meaning of, 34–37
    nurturing, 40–50
    reproducibles for, 52–57
identity
    sense of belonging and, 10, 11
    social justice and, 6, 12, 13
instruction
    customizing, 72
    instructional strategies, 44
introduction
    about behavior and mindsets, 1–2
    navigating this book, 6–7
    parsing the research, 2–3
    taking action to target mindsets, 3–6

J

Jacobson, A., 46–47
journals
    gratitude journals, 17, 49
    measuring student mindsets, 98
    reproducibles for, 27–28

L

Laal, M., 82
learning difficulties, 43–44
learning strategies, 2, 3
learning trackers, 69–72

lifelong learning, 80, 82–83
literature, 42–43
low expectations, 41. *See also expectations*

M

Maslow's hierarchy of needs, 10–11, 33
mastery experiences, 39
meetings, 13–14, 15
mentors, 14
metacognitive skills, use of term, 1
mindsets. *See also "I belong in this academic community" mindset; "I can succeed at this" mindset; "My ability and competence grow with my effort" mindset; "This work has value to me" mindset*
    adult mindsets, 97–98
    categories of behaviors and, 2–3
    measuring student mindsets, 98
    mindset minilessons, 15, 16, 20
    mindset surveys, 98
    taking action to target mindsets, 3–6
minilessons, 15, 16, 20
mission, 63–66
mistakes
    growth mindset and, 85
    as normal and productive, 45–46
motivation, 11, 39, 60
"My ability and competence grow with my effort" mindset. *See also growth mindset*
    about, 79–80
    action items, 89
    focusing on, 83–84
    learning targets, 78
    meaning of, 80–83
    nurturing, 84–89
    reproducibles for, 90–95

N

Ng, B., 86
norms
    cocreating school and classroom norms, visions, missions, and compacts, 63–66
    nurturing a sense of belonging and, 12

P

Pajares, F., 39
Paunesku, D., 39
perseverance, 2, 3
physical education, 43
policy and practice, 42
positive behavioral interventions and supports (PBIS), 5, 64–65
poverty, impact of, 39, 83–84
progress
    definition of, 36
    measuring progress and success, 46–47, 49–50

R

relationships
    student-to-student relationships, 14
    teacher-student relationships, 15–18
relevance, explaining relevance of topic or skills, 66–67. *See also "This work has value to me" mindset*
reproducibles for
    check-in/check-out process, 29
    classroom environment survey, 23–25
    gratitude journal prompts, 27–28
    growth mindset survey for students, 90
    "I belong in this academic community" action plan, 30–31
    "I can succeed at this" action plan, 54–57
    interest and connections survey, 22
    mindfulness exercises, 52–53
    mindset minilesson design, 20
    "My ability and competence grow with my effort" action plan, 94–95
    student growth mindset survey for teachers' assessment, 91–93
    student input on behaviors at recess and lunch, 26
    "This work has value to me" action plan, 75–76
    what I want my teacher to know, 21
resilience, modeling, 88–89
rigor, 45, 80–82
risk taking, 88

S

Schimmer, T., 87
Schlechty, P., 59

Seita, J., 4
SEL (social-emotional learning), 5
SEL calendar, 48
self-efficacy, 11, 38. *See also "I can succeed at this" mindset*
self-regulation, use of term, 1
Sieta, J., 4
Snipes, J., 38
social justice, 6, 12–13
social skills, 2, 3
soft start class times, 13
standards-based grading, 87
status, definition of, 36
student interest surveys, 15–16
student-to-student relationships, 14
success, measuring progress and, 46–47, 49–50. *See also "I can succeed at this" mindset*
surveys
    environmental surveys, 17
    reproducibles for, 21, 22, 23–25, 26, 90, 91–93
    student interest surveys, 15–16

T

teacher-student relationships, 15–18
"This work has value to me" mindset. *See also relevance*
    about, 59
    action items, 73–74
    focusing on, 61–63
    learning targets, 58
    meaning of, 59–61
    nurturing, 63–73
    reproducibles for, 75–76
Three Before Me strategy, 45–46, 85
Tran, L., 38
trauma-informed practices, 5–6

U

Usher, E., 39

V

verbal and social persuasion, 39
vicarious experiences, 39
Virgil, 33
Visible Learning for Teachers: Maximizing Impact on Learning (Hattie), 41
vision, 63–66
voice and choice, 42–43

W

Weber, C., 1

Y

yet
    importance of *yet*, 37
    letting them know (and believing it yourself), 42

Z

zone of proximal development (ZPD), 37, 81

The Road to Success With MTSS
Tom Hierck and Chris Weber
Packed with research-based strategies, The Road to Success With MTSS is an essential road map for educators beginning their school's multitiered system of supports (MTSS) journey and those who have already come so far and are looking to reflect and reset for success.
BKG084

Behavior: The Forgotten Curriculum
Chris Weber
Discover how to fully prepare students for college, careers, and life by nurturing their behavioral skills along with their academic skills. Learn how to employ the most effective behavioral-skill exercises for your particular class and form unique relationships with every learner.
BKF828

Behavior Academies
Jessica Djabrayan Hannigan and John Hannigan
With its practical behavior intervention method, this book replaces problematic behaviors with essential life skills for school and beyond. Educators can implement effective targeted interventions in twenty-five or fewer minutes using eight predefined behavior academies, and learn a process to create their own.
BKG114

Motivated to Learn
Staci M. Zolkoski, Calli Lewis Chiu, and Mandy E. Lusk
In Motivated to Learn, you will gain evidence-based approaches for engaging students and equipping them to better focus in the classroom. With this book's straightforward strategies, you can learn to motivate all your students to actively participate in learning.
BKG037

Solution Tree | Press

Visit SolutionTree.com or call 800.733.6786 to order.

Global PD teams
Collaborative Learning for School Improvement

Quality team learning **from authors you trust**

Global PD Teams is the first-ever **online professional development resource designed to support your entire faculty on your learning journey.** This convenient tool offers daily access to videos, mini-courses, eBooks, articles, and more packed with insights and research-backed strategies you can use immediately.

GET STARTED
SolutionTree.com/**GlobalPDTeams**
800.733.6786